SECRET
BATH
AN UNUSUAL GUIDE

Karen Warren

JONGLEZ PUBLISHING

Travel guides

Karen Warren is a travel writer, novelist and book reviewer based in Bath. She is on a mission to persuade people to look beyond the obvious tourist sights, to scratch beneath the surface and to discover places for themselves. She writes about her travels in search of the interesting and the unusual on her blog WorldWideWriter.

We immensely enjoyed writing the *Secret Bath* guide and hope that, like us, you will continue to discover the unusual, secret and lesser-known facets of this city.

Accompanying the description of some sites, you will find historical information and anecdotes that will let you understand the city in all its complexity.

Secret Bath also sheds light on the numerous yet overlooked details of places we pass by every day. These details are an invitation to pay more attention to the urban landscape and, more generally, to regard our city with the same curiosity and attention we often feel when travelling.

Comments on this guide and its contents, as well as information on sites not mentioned, are welcome and will help us to enrich future editions.

Don't hesitate to contact us:
Email: info@jonglezpublishing.com

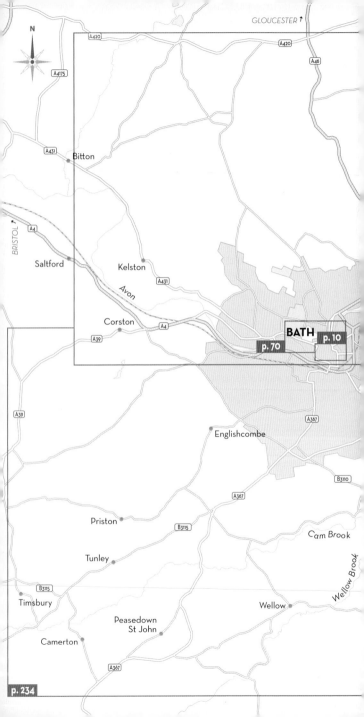

N

GLOUCESTER ↑

A420

A420

A46

A4175

A431

Bitton

BRISTOL ↑

A4

A431

Saltford

Kelston

Avon

Corston

A4

A39

BATH

p. 70

p. 10

A39

Englishcombe

A367

B3110

Priston

B3115

A367

Cam Brook

Tunley

Wellow Brook

B3115

Timsbury

Wellow

Peasedown
St John

Camerton

A367

p. 234

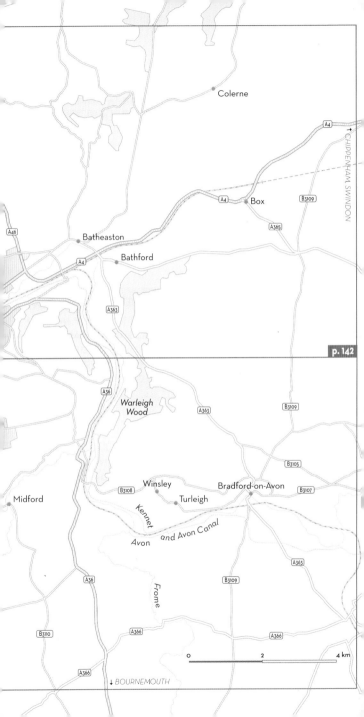

Colerne

↑ CHIPPENHAM SWINDON

A4

A4   Box

B3109

A365

A46

Batheaston

A4   Bathford

A363

p. 142

A36

Warleigh Wood

A363

B3109

B3105

B3108   Winsley

Bradford-on-Avon   B3107

Midford

Turleigh

Kennet

and Avon Canal

Avon

A363

A36

Frome

B3109

B3110   A366

A366

0   2   4 km

A366

↓ BOURNEMOUTH

CONTENTS

South

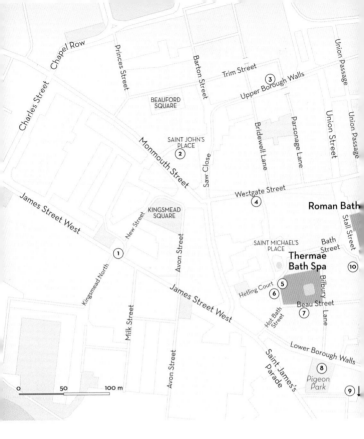

Lower Town

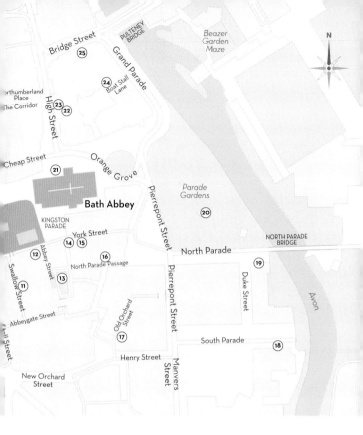

OLD LABOUR EXCHANGE ①

Memorial to victims of the Bath Blitz

Junction of James Street West and Kingsmead North, BA1 2BX

Some of the city's buildings that were bombed in the Second World War have now disappeared altogether. Others have been carefully rebuilt in their original form. But the old Labour Exchange has made a feature of its damage. Its wartime scars are still visible and the building bears a memorial to the victims of the Bath Blitz.

At the start of the war, Bath was relatively untouched apart from a few stray bombs from planes on their way to Bristol. The Germans were aware of the new military airfield at Charmy Down (see p. 208) but it seems that they did not know about the local factories manufacturing weapons and aircraft parts. So the city was not seen as an obvious target.

That all changed in 1942 with the so-called Baedeker Raids. As a response to the RAF bombing of civilian targets, including the historic city of Lübeck, the Germans planned a series of raids on British cities known for their architectural importance. The cities targeted were thought to have been chosen from the Baedeker guides, a series of German tourist handbooks.

Over the course of a single weekend (25–27 April 1942), 417 people were killed in Bath and some 1,000 injured. Many buildings were destroyed or damaged, including homes, churches and important Georgian buildings such as the Assembly Rooms.

The Labour Exchange, which also acted as a centre for civil defence during the war, was severely damaged in the raids. It suffered shrapnel damage from the bombing of the nearby Holy Trinity Church, and a second bomb the following day set the building on fire, destroying the roof and the top floor.

Despite the damage, the Labour Exchange continued with its essential functions, assisting those who had lost their homes and helping people to find work in support of the war effort. It fell out of use after the war but members of the Bath Blitz Memorial Project campaigned to preserve the building as a reminder of that terrible weekend.

The upper floors were eventually rebuilt and the building reopened as a mixed student accommodation and commercial space. But two sides of the ground floor are still covered with shrapnel marks. In 2016 a memorial plaque was added, telling the story of the Labour Exchange and honouring the memory of those who died in the Bath Blitz.

HAND FOUNTAIN AT SEVEN DIALS ②

Where actors left their mark

Inner courtyard of Seven Dials, BA1 1EN

Few people seem to be aware of the small courtyard at the centre of Seven Dials unless they have eaten at one of the restaurants around the edge. Those that do visit may notice a rather overgrown fountain with bronze handprints around the edge.

Seven Dials was once a much more important area than it is now. Just outside the historic west gate of the city, it was the point where seven roads met. However, the Georgian buildings at the centre suffered wartime bomb damage and the site subsequently became rather neglected.

The renovation of the adjacent Theatre Royal provided an opportunity to consider the future of Seven Dials. In 1991 the architects Aaron Evans were commissioned to design a neoclassical triangular building with a central courtyard. This was to be used as a mixed restaurant, shopping and office space.

The courtyard needed a centrepiece and a Victorian fountain was sourced from the Bath firm Walcot Reclamation (who were incidentally one of the early pioneers of the architectural salvage business, founded in 1976 but sadly no longer trading). Because of the proximity of the theatre, it was decided to emulate the example of the Chinese Theatre in Hollywood, where hand- and footprints of famous actors are set into the pavement outside.

There was no room for footprints but 16 actors who had appeared at the Theatre Royal were persuaded to have casts taken of their hands and to add their signatures. The names include Penelope Keith, Derek Jacobi and Hayley Mills.

Once the work was completed, Seven Dials was sold. Unfortunately, the new owners decided that they had no interest in maintaining a water feature and replaced the running water with a flowerbed. The handprints remain, however – a reminder of past theatrical performances.

Walk out of Seven Dials to the corner opposite the Theatre Royal and you'll see a cylindrical metal structure covered in advertising posters. Although it looks like a purpose-built billboard, it's actually a vent for the electricity substation below.

CITY WALL AND BURIAL GROUND ③

Part of the old city walls

Upper Borough Walls, BA1 1HB

In the Middle Ages, Bath was one of the smallest walled cities in England. The walls enclosed the town created by King Alfred in the 9th century and probably followed the line of the earlier Roman fortifications. A small fragment of the wall is still visible on the appropriately named Upper Borough Walls, and behind it are the remnants of an old cemetery.

Although many of the city centre streets still follow the route of their Saxon predecessors, the walls that enclosed them were pulled down in the 18th century to make room for the Georgian building boom, leaving only small fragments. So you might ask why this small section was allowed to remain and wonder why it should have been rebuilt and reconstructed in the Victorian era.

If you walk down the steps behind the wall you'll see some of the original medieval stonework. You will also understand why this part of the wall stayed standing: it formed the boundary of a burial ground.

The unfortunate people who were buried here were patients from the Royal Mineral Water Hospital (see below), on the opposite side of the road. Some were cured and returned home; others died and were brought to the burial ground.

The graveyard closed in 1849, partly because it was full and partly due to public health concerns. The area at the back of the wall and a small plaque are all that now remain.

For more information about the city walls, and the remaining fragments, see the following double-page spread.

Royal Mineral Water Hospital

The hospital was built by John Wood the Elder between 1738 and 1742. It was a charitable enterprise: Wood did not charge for his work and the institution was intended to cater for the sick – but penniless – pilgrims who visited Bath to take the waters.

The grand neoclassical building closed as a hospital some years ago and there are now plans to turn it into a hotel. But you can still admire the building from the outside. Look out for the carving of the Good Samaritan beneath the roof of the Victorian extension (just opposite the remains of the city wall).

Remains of Bath city walls

From Roman times until the Civil War in the 17th century, walls were essential for the defence of the city. The first walls were built by the Romans in the 3rd century CE and later provided the foundations for the Saxon defences. In the 12th century, during a period of civil unrest, King Stephen ordered the height of the walls to be increased.

The walls included four gates, of which only the Eastgate (see p. 66) now survives. The north and south gates were topped by statues, with King Edward III on the south gate and King Bladud on the north gate (this may have been the same statue that is now in the Roman Baths – see p. 33).

The walls seem to have remained intact for many centuries. The diarist Samuel Pepys visited Bath in 1668 and noted that he had walked all around the walls. But by the 18th century they had become an impediment to new development and they were gradually demolished.

Although the walls have now almost disappeared, you can still see evidence of their route around the city in the street names. Upper Borough Walls and Lower Borough Walls mark the northern and southern limits of the town. And the entrances into the city are indicated by Westgate Street, Southgate Street and Northgate Street.

Most of what remains of the walls is now built into the foundations of later buildings or hidden away in basements. However, apart from the sections on Upper Borough Walls (see p. 16) and at the Eastgate, there is one other significant fragment to find.

This is probably the least-known part of the wall as it is hidden away behind the Marks & Spencer's delivery bay, close to Old Orchard Street. Until 1959 this was a very substantial piece of masonry but it was mostly demolished to allow for building work. However, a large section remains, standing 6 metres high. The base is believed to be Roman.

If you search hard enough, you can find still more evidence of the old city walls elsewhere. Go into the Guildhall Market and look for a strip of polished stone on the floor of a hardware stall: this is said to mark the route of the wall. And stand outside the Abbey Hotel and peer down into the basement area to see a small section of wall disappearing into the building's foundations.

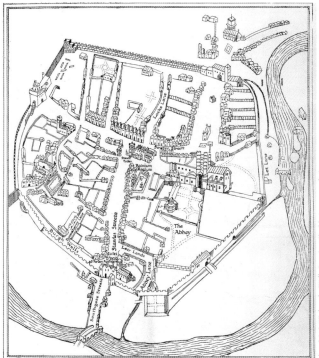

1600s MAP Within the Walls Rev CW Shickle (courtesy of Akeman Press)

POCOCK'S LIVING ROOM

④

A well-preserved Jacobean room

The Grapes, 14 Westgate Street, BA1 1EQ
thegrapesbath.co.uk
Open for events: see website for details

The Grapes is renowned as being an 'eclectic' pub, with live music, craft beers and real ale. Perhaps less well known is that it is housed in one of the oldest surviving buildings in Bath. And that its upstairs events space is a lovingly preserved Jacobean room.

Although there has been a building on this site since the Middle Ages, the current structure is an Elizabethan town house with later additions. It was originally a private home, possibly owned by Richard Gay, the mayor of Bath. However it later seems to have catered for the tourists who were starting to flock to the city for the benefit of their health. A late 17th-century map of Bath describes the property as 'Ms Pococks Lodgings in West Gate Street'.

It later became a wine merchant and around 1800 it opened as a pub, originally called The Bunch of Grapes. Now simply renamed The Grapes, the building is a bar and entertainment venue and has also reclaimed its earlier function as a hotel, its upper rooms refurbished in period style.

It isn't until you go up to what is now known as Pocock's Living Room that you appreciate exactly how old The Grapes is. This room, which would once have been the main sitting room, has been restored to its original splendour, an ornate room with elaborate and expensive ornamentation.

The most striking feature of the Jacobean Room is the plasterwork ceiling, added in 1612. This is the oldest remaining plasterwork in Bath, with intricate detail including heraldic devices. Interestingly, almost identical fragments of plaster have recently been discovered beneath the floor of Bath Abbey, likely to have been the work of the same person.

There are lots of opportunities to see Pocock's Living Room for yourself as it hosts a wide variety of events. You'll find life-drawing classes and folk music evenings here as well as community meetings and private parties. The Jacobean Room is as lively now as it would have been in Ms Pocock's time!

KING EDGAR AND OLD
KING COLE STATUES

The forgotten statues of two medieval kings

Bath Street, BA1 1SJ

Squeezed between the Hot Bath and the entrance to the Thermae Bath Spa is one of the narrowest buildings in the city. Above the door are two niches, filled with somewhat battered and almost forgotten statues: King Edgar and King Coel (also known as King Cole).

The building itself was once the Museum of Antiquities, built in 1797 by John Palmer to house artefacts discovered during 18th-century excavations in Bath. This was possibly one of the earliest archaeological museums in England, but it did not survive; we are told that it later became the home of the Master of the Baths.

The origins of the statues are obscure. They are thought to have been created in the 15th century and may once have stood on one of the bridges across the Avon. What we do know is that at one time they sat on the outside of Bath's 'Stuart Guildhall' of 1625, the second of the city's three guildhalls. They were removed in 1766 when the current Guildhall was built and found their way to the Museum of Antiquities.

But who were King Edgar and King Coel and what was their connection with Bath? King Edgar is easier to understand: he is a contender for the title of 'first king of all England' and ruled the country from 959 to 975. Whether or not Edgar was actually the first king, he certainly seems to have been the first to have been formally crowned: his coronation took place in Bath's Abbey Church in 973. This ceremony is said to have set the format for all subsequent coronations, right up to the present day.

King Coel, on the other hand, is probably best known today as the subject of the nursery rhyme 'Old King Cole', but who he really was is a bit of a mystery. He might have been a 5th-century king of Northern Britain. Or he might have been a king (almost certainly fictitious) based in Colchester, who became the grandfather of the Roman emperor Constantine.

Either way, there seems to be little truth in the claim that King Coel lived in Bath. It is even doubtful whether he has any connection with the city at all, apart from a slightly crumbling statue.

BATH MEDICAL MUSEUM

Exploring the city's medical history

Hetling Pump Room, Hot Bath Street, BA1 1SJ
bathmedicalmuseum.org
See website for visiting times

Oone way or another, the history of Bath is tied up with the history of medicine. The Romans came here for the healing waters, as did the Georgians, and even today wellness is part of the city's tourist offering. The Bath Medical Museum's mission is to record and share that heritage.

The museum has had a varied history. It opened in 2012 with an extensive collection of medical artefacts and artworks housed in the Royal Mineral Water Hospital. The hospital (see p. 17) was a historic site for medical treatment in the city centre. When it was sold in 2019, the museum became homeless.

Some items were relocated to other local museums while others were put into storage. The museum's online offering allowed people to explore some of the collection and to take a virtual tour of the Mineral Hospital. In 2023 new premises were found at the Hetling Pump Room, where people once drank the healing waters from the Hetling Spring, one of the three main springs in Bath.

Although the museum continues to collaborate with other local bodies and to provide outreach and learning facilities, the relocation to the Hetling Pump Room has enabled the creation of a small exhibition and events space. There are several information boards, which tell of the Spa Quarter of Bath and the city's medical history, from Bladud and his pigs (see p. 58) to the modern-day spa revival.

Then there is a variety of medical artefacts. These are likely to change from time to time, but a recent display included a large metal contraption known as a 'needle douche'. This was a device for pointing sharp jets of water at the patient and, despite its primitive appearance, it remained in use until 1976. (The douche later featured as a prop in the 1985 James Bond film, *A View to a Kill*.) Other exhibits included a display of 'International aspects of wellbeing', with items such as Tibetan meditation cymbals. And there were family-friendly displays and activities.

The Bath Medical Museum is occasionally open for events and activities. It can also be visited by appointment. See the website for details.

(The needle douche in the picture was on loan from The Roman Baths, Bath and North East Somerset Council collection.)

BEAU STREET HOARD

A remarkable archaeological discovery

Gainsborough Bath Spa Hotel
Beau Street, BA1 1QY
thegainsboroughbathspa.co.uk
Visible in reception area at any reasonable time

The Gainsborough Bath Spa Hotel is a luxury hotel with a spa which is – uniquely – fed by the city's hot springs. However, that is not its only distinction: it is also the site of one of the major archaeological discoveries to have been made anywhere in the city. And you can see some of what was found in a display case in the hotel's reception area.

The Gainsborough occupies two 18th-century buildings that were originally built as the Royal United Hospital and Bellot's Hospital, designed to take advantage of the local healing waters. An excavation in 1864 revealed that the hospitals had been built upon an old Roman spa complex. But it was not until the site was being converted into a hotel in 2007 that the real discovery was made.

Archaeologists found eight money-bags secreted beneath the floor. These held an incredible total of 17,660 Roman coins, believed to have been hidden here around 275 CE. The oldest coin in the collection dates from 31 or 32 BCE.

The Beau Street Hoard – as it became known – is the fifth-largest hoard of coins ever found in Britain. It is also the largest to have been unearthed in a British Roman town, as hoards have more usually been found in rural locations.

As with all such discoveries, we don't really know why the coins were hidden or why the original owners did not return to claim what would have been a vast amount of money, possibly built up over a period of time. We can only speculate as to who owned the money and what happened to them.

Most of the coins are now on display at the Roman Baths Museum. However, some of the hoard was allowed to remain in the hotel premises and is now proudly displayed in a glass case to the right of the main entrance.

A Roman mosaic

The archaeologists also found a Victorian time capsule and a 4th-century Roman mosaic that had first been discovered during the 1864 excavation. The original mosaic remains below ground but an exact replica can be seen in the hotel's spa area.

ROADPEACE MEMORIAL

Remembering lives lost on the roads

Pigeon Park, Lower Borough Walls, BA1 1QR

For many people, Pigeon Park is just a city centre thoroughfare, a shortcut between Lower Borough Walls and St James's Parade. Few stop to look at the inscribed stone beside the path, a memorial to local victims of road accidents.

The triangular sculpture is built from textured Bath stone. Beneath the inscription – 'Remembering lives lost and broken on our roads in the South West' – are carved ivy leaves. And above is a black marble circle etched with the symbol of a dove and a line of road markings beneath its wings.

This symbol is the logo of RoadPeace, a national charity founded in 1992 with the aim of reducing road deaths and supporting the bereaved. The charity also aims to remember those who have died on the roads, by means of physical and online memorials, religious services and other remembrance ceremonies.

Designed by Rebecca Yeo and sculpted by Yannick Yi Ah Kane, the Pigeon Park memorial was commissioned by the South West RoadPeace Group. It was unveiled in 2010 in a ceremony that included songs by the Bathwick Church Choir, a two-minute silence and the release of seven white doves. The number seven represented both the seven counties of the South West and the average number of lives lost on the roads every day.

Pigeon Park: a medieval place of execution for witches?

Apart from the RoadPeace memorial, Pigeon Park appears to be a rather featureless patch of ground. However, its location just outside the old city walls has ensured a long and varied history.

It was once a burial ground for the old St James Church, which was destroyed by wartime bombing. More colourfully, it is claimed that this was a medieval place of execution and that many witches met their end here. In the 15th century one such witch cursed the ground, a way of ensuring that no one ever dared to build a house on the site.

In 1780 the area was the scene of the Gordon Riots, a massive anti-Catholic protest that started in London but spread elsewhere. In Bath, a mob descended upon a newly built Catholic church and burnt it to the ground. Perhaps the witch's curse had come true!

THE FORUM

An art deco events space in the Georgian city

1A Forum Buildings, St James's Parade, BA1 1UG
bathforum.co.uk
Events and Sunday church services at 10.30am

Bath is well known for its architecture, but you might be surprised to find an art deco cinema nestling among the more traditional buildings. You might not even spot The Forum at first, with its neoclassical Bath stone exterior blending into its surroundings. But go inside and you'll find an interior unlike any other in the city.

The Forum cinema opened in 1934. It was a luxurious venue, sumptuously decorated in the then fashionable art deco style. It could accommodate up to 2,000 people, making it the largest venue in Bath. It is easy to imagine the excitement as people queued to watch the latest films in splendid surroundings. This was at the height of the Great Depression, and the new cinema must have offered a welcome form of escapism.

The Forum remained a popular venue for more than three decades, until the last film was shown in 1969. It was then used as a bingo hall, ballroom and dance school. The building was eventually purchased by the Bath City Church in 1988, and renovated in a manner sympathetic to the original design. It now hosts commercial events and Sunday church services.

The art deco interior is remarkably well-preserved, making this one of the few remaining buildings of its type in Britain. The auditorium has a balcony, chandeliers, and a massive ceiling dome. A classical frieze runs around the edge, and brightly coloured ornamental panels adorn the walls and ceiling. Beside the auditorium is the old ballroom, once a place for dancing but now used as a bar during events.

The Forum is home to numerous activities, including concerts and comedy performances. Some events from the Bath festivals take place here, as well as occasional private functions. And everyone is welcome at the Bath City Church, which has a service here on Sunday mornings at 10.30am.

THE KING'S LOUNGE

A little-known view of the King's Bath

Roman Baths, Stall Street entrance, BA1 1LZ
Daily, 10am–5pm
Entrance free

The queues outside the Roman Baths attest to the fact that this is one of the most visited tourist attractions in the country. But did you know that you can look down upon one of the oldest parts of the baths from a secluded area that few people seem to be aware of?

Enter via the ornate Stall Street entrance – beneath the heading 'King's and Queen's Baths' – and ask to visit the King's Lounge. This is a small room to the left, just beside the Pump Room.

The room itself is not particularly grand, apart from a single chandelier hanging from the ceiling. It is mostly used as a bar for the many private functions that take place within the Roman Baths. But daytime visitors can look through the windows for one of the best – and certainly quietest – views of the King's Bath.

Built in the 12th century, the King's Bath was one of three medieval baths created from the remains of the Roman complex. This is the site of the King's Spring, which feeds the Great Bath, and it is remarkably unchanged since early times.

You will spot some semicircular windows on the right-hand side. This is where Roman bathers would throw their 'curse tablets' into the water. These were thin sheets of lead or pewter upon which aggrieved citizens would describe the wrongs that had been done to them and specify the revenge they wished to wreak upon the perpetrators. They would then roll up the curses and toss them into the spring for the attention of the goddess Sulis Minerva!

Also on the right-hand side is a statue of King Bladud, the legendary founder of Bath, who supposedly discovered the healing waters in 863 BCE. This statue might have been the one that stood on the city's North Gate prior to its demolition in 1755.

Before leaving the King's Lounge, have a look at the displays on the walls. One side has information about the King's Bath with some of the artefacts found here, including coins and a curse tablet. The opposite wall is used for temporary exhibitions; past subjects have included the Emperor Haile Selassie (see p. 156) and spa treatments in Bath.

How high was the water in Victorian times?

Look closely at the King's Bath and you'll see a rusty stain around the walls, caused by iron in the water. This shows how high the water was in Victorian times before it was taken back down to the Roman level.

LAUNDRY CHIMNEY

An industrial relic in the heart of the city

Swallow Street, BA1 1NP

Although it's in the city centre, few people seem to walk along Swallow Street, a slightly dingy road leading away from the Roman Baths. Even fewer look up at the rooftops, but those who do may be surprised to see a tall, ornate chimney. This is one of the few visible remains of what was once an important part of Bath's spa activity: the City Laundry.

The laundry was built in the late 19th century. At that time many people visited the spa for healing purposes and huge amounts of clothes and towels needed to be washed. The laundry later also dealt with items belonging to the city council, including washroom roller towels and staff overalls. Up to half a million items were laundered here every year.

It made sense to site the laundry close to the Baths, where there was an abundant natural source of hot water. However, the boilers and washing machines were powered by coal, which generated a vast amount of smoke.

A tall chimney was needed to carry the smoke away. As seems to have been typical of Victorian industrial structures, the chimney was elaborate, a massive construction of fluted limestone ashlar standing on a large arcaded base.

The laundry finally closed in 1976. The building has now been converted into the city's World Heritage Centre, introducing visitors to Bath's two UNESCO listings (a World Heritage Site and one of the Great Spa Towns of Europe). There is little to remind you of the laundry in the centre itself although a skylight in the upper floor looks up to the chimney shaft.

Unfortunately, this area is restricted to school and community groups but it is occasionally accessible on Heritage Open Days. However, the chimney itself remains visible to anyone who cares to walk past and look up.

You may have wondered about the arch above York Street that spans the space between the Baths and the World Heritage Centre. This was originally built to hold the pipes that carried hot water to the laundry. Stop to look at the decorative heads carved onto the arch and see if you can spot two dogs' heads. They are said to have been modelled on the architect's own dog!

Bath as a World Heritage Site: a rare example of a city with two separate UNESCO inscriptions

Since 1978 UNESCO has designated hundreds of places around the world as World Heritage Sites. These are places of exceptional cultural or natural heritage, regarded as being of 'outstanding universal value to humanity'.

Bath is a rare example of a city with two separate UNESCO inscriptions. In 1987 the City of Bath was added to the list of World Heritage Sites and it featured again in 2021 as part of the Great Spa Towns of Europe.

The City of Bath was one of the UK's earliest UNESCO sites, an indication of its national as well as international importance. A further distinction is that Bath is one of only two entire cities to be inscribed as World Heritage Sites (the other is Venice).

Every World Heritage Site has one or more natural or cultural criteria for inclusion in the list – Bath has six! As you might expect, one of these is the city's Roman Baths, described by UNESCO as 'amongst the most famous and important Roman remains north of the Alps'.

The Georgian city contributes three separate criteria. First, there is the neoclassical architecture with its distinctive pattern of crescents, squares and terraces all built from the local Bath stone. This leads on to 18th-century town planning and the way that the city was redesigned to take advantage of the natural landscape and the development of Bath as a fashionable resort.

The other legacy of the Georgian period is the social setting. For many wealthy people, a season in Bath became part of the social calendar and many writers, artists and other prominent people were regular visitors. Largely due to the influence of Beau Nash, the official Master of Ceremonies, Bath led the way in setting the rules for polite society.

Then there is the green setting. Bath lies in a valley surrounded by hills, with views of the countryside in all directions. The city has a river, a canal and numerous parks.

The final criterion relates to the hot springs. The source of Bath's importance in both Roman and Georgian times, these are the only natural hot springs in Britain, emerging from the ground at a temperature of 45°C (elsewhere in the country, springs reach a lower temperature and are merely 'warm').

It was these springs, together with the city's spa culture, that led to Bath's second UNESCO inscription, as part of the Great Spa Towns of Europe, listings that so far include 11 towns in 7 different countries. These towns were all at the forefront of social, medical and architectural development between the 18th and 20th centuries and they were sometimes known as the 'cafés of Europe'. Like Bath, all these spa towns took advantage of their natural setting as well as their built environment. And they are part of a living tradition, continuing to promote health and well-being.

To explore Bath's UNESCO status further, go into the World Heritage Centre on York Street. And look out for the World Heritage emblem as you walk around the city: you'll find it on the ground opposite the end of Stall Street and engraved onto a door outside the railway station. The square represents human skill and inspiration while the circle celebrates the gifts of nature. These are all characteristics to be found in abundance here.

THE CITY OF BATH - WORLD HERITAGE SITE

The World Heritage Symbol commemorates the inscription by UNESCO of The City of Bath on the World Heritage List in 1987. This identifies the city as a masterpiece of human creative genius whose protection must be the concern of all.

44AD ARTSPACE

An independent art space in the city centre

4 Abbey Street, BA1 1NN
44ad.net
See website for opening times

Tucked away in a Georgian house on the corner of Abbey Street, 44AD is often overlooked by visitors on their way to the Abbey or the Roman Baths. But those who venture inside will find a thriving contemporary art space with regularly changing exhibitions.

44AD was established in 2012. The aim was to provide inclusive and cost-effective studio facilities for local artists and to give them a place to exhibit their work. It now has three floors of studio space and a ground-floor exhibition area. The basement is a flexible space and can be used for workshops, talks or exhibitions.

The gallery is a community enterprise, run as a charity. This means that, while some artists rent their studios on a long-term basis, residencies are offered to newly graduated students. They are offered a studio, materials and an exhibition of their work; in return, they are asked to give talks and workshops. The gallery also hosts art competitions and liaises with local schools and other groups within the community.

But this is not just a place for artists. Members of the public are welcome to visit the exhibitions, which change on a weekly basis and showcase the work of the studio residents and other local artists.

As well as the exhibitions there are regular talks and workshops, and occasional 'open studios' where you can meet the artists and discuss their work. Opening times for the gallery vary but it is usually open from Tuesday to Saturday. Details are on the website.

Where did the name 44AD come from? You might think that it's a reference to the arrival of the Romans in Britain, but that was one year earlier. There is definitely a Roman connection, however. Before it moved to its current location, the gallery was housed in a property opposite the former St James' Chapel in Pigeon Park (see p. 29) and it took its name from the date of St James' martyrdom. This is particularly appropriate as the current premises overlook the Roman Baths and a statue of Claudius. And Claudius was emperor at the time that St James was put to death …

LONDON PLANE TREE

One of the oldest architecturally planted trees in the world

Abbey Green, BA1 1NR

Passers-by may stand beneath the shade of the gigantic London plane in Abbey Green without realising that this tree – remarkable in its own right – is the subject of several mysteries.

The first mystery concerns its age. No one disputes that it is very old, but when exactly was it planted? Some sources say that it arrived as a sapling in 1793, others that it was planted following a change of ownership of the land in 1894.

Both dates are possible as London pines are a long-lived species. Either way, this is one of the oldest architecturally planted trees in the world. It is also very large, dominating the small square in which it stands. Of course, this is partly due to its great age but it is also possible that it is fed by natural springs, its roots reaching down to the water beneath the nearby Roman Baths.

Ghosts and apparitions

Another mystery surrounding the plane tree is that ghosts are said to haunt the area. The naked Roman legionary and the hooded monks are perhaps easy to understand: Roman remains have been found in the adjacent Crystal Palace pub and medieval monks would have walked through the green on their way to the Abbey. Although no one has explained how we can identify a ghost as a Roman if he is naked … More enigmatic is the reported appearance of a figure hanging from the tree. Stories persist that it was once used as a gallows and it is even known as the 'Hanging Tree'. However this is extremely unlikely, even if it was planted in 1793. It is hard to see how it could have grown large and strong enough for the purpose before public executions were finally abolished. Of course there might have been an earlier hanging tree on the same spot. Another legend says that there is a patch of ground beneath the tree where nothing will grow, perhaps as the result of an ancient curse. However, we can no longer tell if this is true. The area around the tree was paved over and covered with gravel in 2017. So that is one secret the tree will have to keep.

Visitors to Bath may find that Abbey Green, and the tree at its centre, looks very familiar. This is because the green has been used as a location for many film and TV productions. Most recently it appeared in *Bridgerton*, where the square stood in for London's Covent Garden. The Abbey Deli, on the side of the green, became the Modiste dress shop.

MASONIC SYMBOLS AT THE OLD FRIENDS MEETING HOUSE

A reminder of the building's original purpose

Topping & Company
York Street, BA1 1NG

Stand outside Topping's bookshop on York Street and look up at the cast-iron rainwater spouts on the side elevations. You'll see that they are more than purely functional items: each is decorated with the symbol of a square and compasses.

This ornamentation is a reminder of the building's early history. For many years, from 1866 until the 1980s, it was the home of the Society of Friends (or Quakers); it only became a bookshop in 2021. However, when it first opened in 1819 it was a Masonic hall, a meeting place for the local lodges.

Freemasonry was an important part of Bath society in the 18th century and it was here that the first lodge outside of London opened in 1724. Beau Nash, the Master of Ceremonies, was certainly a Freemason, and it is thought that other prominent citizens, including Ralph Allen and John Wood the Elder, were also members of the society.

The square and compasses that still survive outside the former meeting house are a universally recognised symbol of Freemasonry. The meaning is multilayered, invoking both the intricate skill of the mason's work and the esoteric practice of the Freemasons.

The stonemason would use a square to check that the angles of a building were correct, and thus the square became associated both with matter (the stone) and with rectitude. This linked in with the Masonic principles of morality and virtue.

The compasses are another tool that would have been used by the mason, this time for drawing arcs and circles. These are an essential part of architecture and symbolise the mind and spirit. However, they also represent boundaries, thus invoking the important concept of self-restraint.

The square and compasses are often used together but their relative position is also important, demonstrating the relationship between matter and mind (or spirit). Where, as is the case in the old Friends Meeting House, they are crossed over one another, this shows that mind and matter are equally balanced (see below).

There are two other possible positions for the square and compasses. If the square is placed on top, this indicates that matter is taking precedence over spirit: this is the first degree (or Entered Apprentice stage) of Freemasonry. However, if the compasses are above the square, then the spirit has overcome matter and the practitioner has progressed to the third grade of Master Mason.

The distinctive Greek Revival exterior of Topping's bookshop is a rarity in Bath. Another curious feature – reflecting its Freemason design – is that the building originally featured a blind door and windows. This ensured secrecy but was also symbolic, suggesting that 'the way to enlightenment is not always obvious'. The Masonic date 5819 (representing 1819 in the Gregorian calendar) was shown above the doorway. When you go inside the shop, stop to admire the way that the cavernous meeting room has been transformed into floor-to-ceiling bookshelves. Note also the original circular roof lanterns.

FACADE OF RALPH ALLEN'S TOWN HOUSE

(15)

Catch a glimpse of a magnificent city-centre house, almost hidden from view

2 North Parade Passage, BA1 1NX
View at any time from the passageway beside the Huntsman pub
or via a side door from Topping's bookshop during opening hours

Although Ralph Allen's town house in the centre of Bath still exists, you could walk past it without knowing because its main feature – the grand facade – is almost hidden from view. The part you see is the featureless back of the building on Church Street, looking like what it actually is: a forlorn and rather neglected office block.

In 1727, Allen commissioned John Wood the Elder (the architect responsible for many of Bath's Georgian buildings, including The Circus) to remodel the Post House, the office building from which he ran his business. Wood added a new facade and a north wing to create an elaborate town house. Apart from providing office and living accommodation, the redesigned structure was intended to showcase the stone from Allen's quarries.

The north wing has gone (demolished to create what is now York Street) and what remains of the house is hemmed in by the surrounding buildings. Yet the ornate frontage, built in the Palladian style, with Corinthian columns, sash windows and a decorative pediment, remains. A plaque on the side of the house – now virtually impossible to spot – reads: 'Here lived Ralph Allen 1727–1764'.

Until 2021 the only way to get a glimpse of the facade was to squeeze past the bins on the passageway to the right of the Huntsman pub on Terrace Walk. However, the opening of the new Topping's Bookshop on York Street has provided another option: during opening hours, you can go downstairs and walk through a side door to stand in a small courtyard in front of Ralph Allen's almost forgotten town house.

SALLY LUNN'S KITCHEN MUSEUM

Remains of a medieval monastery

4 North Parade Passage, BA1 1NX
sallylunns.co.uk/kitchen-museum
Sun–Fri 10am–4pm, Sat 10am–6pm
Very small entrance charge, but free to diners

Sally Lunn's Historic Eating House is well known as the oldest house in Bath, the home of Sally Lunn's famous buns and a place for tourists to eat those buns in a quirky environment. What is less familiar is the tiny museum in the basement, where you can step back into the building's medieval past.

When the Georgian city of Bath was built in the 18th century, the street level was artificially raised so that the ground floors of existing buildings became cellars. Many of these are now lost, or bricked up, but at Sally Lunn's you can still stand in the original medieval building. You can even look through a window at the back and see fragments of earlier Roman masonry, yet another level down.

Although the four-storeyed Sally Lunn's tea room was built in 1622, we know that the basement beneath it was part of the priory attached to Bath Abbey until its dissolution in 1539. The date shown outside is 1482, but it is likely that a building stood here much earlier.

Various stories have grown up around the building over the years. The existence of an old – possibly medieval – oven has led to speculation that it was once part of the monastery kitchens. Somewhat less likely is the suggestion that King John ate bread baked in this kitchen in 1207.

Whatever its origins, the museum now displays a kitchen of the past, with a Georgian range and a model of Sally Lunn baking a batch of buns. (In case you're wondering, the semi-legendary Sally Lunn may – or may not – have been a Huguenot refugee from France who brought the recipe for the distinctive buns with her.)

Behind the museum area you can look through a window to an open subterranean space where stalactites have started to form. On a wall is a (probably relatively recent) carving of a pig's head recalling the legend of Bladud, the founder of Bath (see p. 58).

OLD THEATRE ROYAL

The theatre that became a church that became a Masonic lodge

12 Old Orchard Street, BA1 1JU
01225 462233
oldtheatreroyal.com
Tours available several times a week: see website for details

From the outside it doesn't look like much. Apart from a plaque stating that Sarah Siddons – along with other noted 18th-century actors – once appeared here, there is nothing to indicate what lies behind the walls of the Old Theatre Royal. But step inside and you'll find layers of hidden history, a fascinating building and a rather esoteric museum of Freemasonry.

The Old Theatre Royal was built in 1768. However, it fell out of use when the New Theatre Royal, which was closer to the new houses of Georgian Bath, opened in 1805. The theatre building was taken over by the Benedictine Mission in Bath and converted to a place of worship with a burial space in the basement.

In a further change of use, the building was acquired by the Freemasons in 1866. Today there are several Masonic lodges based in the Old Theatre Royal. The theatre is used for ritual dramas and there is a small collection of Masonic medals and other artefacts. The venue also hosts weddings and public performances.

If you attend an event at the Old Theatre Royal, you'll probably find yourself in the original 18th-century theatre, remarkable for its blue star-studded ceiling. For the full experience, however, you need to join one of the tours that are offered several times a week. They will take you behind the scenes to see religious paintings, remnants of the church, catacombs and gravestones.

Most intriguing, however, is the Masonic history, both past and present. The building and its contents are imbued with symbolism. You will hear about the 'personal journey' of Freemasonry and the ways in which even simple objects are used to extract meaning that people can apply to their lives. It feels like a completely different world …

OUR LADY OF BATH, QUEEN OF PEACE STATUE

The largest single block of stone in Bath

St John the Evangelist's Church, South Parade, BA2 4AF
stjohnsrcbath.org.uk
Garden open 8am–5pm

Hidden behind the Church of St John the Evangelist on South Parade is a small riverside garden. The centrepiece of that garden is a remarkable statue of Our Lady of Bath, Queen of Peace.

For many years the land between the church and the river was neglected and overgrown. But in 2017 the church and a group of volunteers decided to restore the garden for the benefit of the local community, visitors to Bath and 'all the natural inhabitants'. Flowers and shrubs were planted and bees and butterflies were coaxed back to the area.

As part of this initiative, a statue of the Virgin Mary was commissioned from the contemporary sculptor Ben Dearnley in 2018. This was to be known as *Our Lady of Bath, Queen of Peace*, in anticipation of the re-dedication of England as the Dowry of our Lady by the Roman Catholic Church in 2020. (England was originally dedicated to Mary by King Richard II in 1381 and 'set apart for her among the nations'.)

The statue was carved from a massive 7.5 tonne block, making it the largest piece of stone in the city. You might be surprised to discover that this is white Portland stone specially transported for the purpose rather than the more familiar golden Bath stone.

Unusually, the sculpture was carved in situ. Over the course of 13 weeks during a hot summer, Dearnley brought his statue to life, often attracting an audience who were keen to watch him at work.

The finished piece is more than 2 metres high. It shows Mary in a long, flowing robe with a veil upon her head, her arms open wide in a gesture of welcome to all-comers. Her downcast eyes and bare feet are symbols of humility.

Mary now dominates the garden, a peaceful space at the back of the church. Visitors are welcome when the garden is open during daytime hours.

Completed in 1863, the Church of St John the Evangelist is an imposing Victorian Gothic building with a tall spire. Inside the church you'll find some impressive stained glass, a delicately wrought-iron rood screen and marble pillars topped with elaborate carvings.

The church is also known for its nesting peregrine falcons, which have made their home in the spire.

DELIA'S GROTTO

Where star-crossed lovers met

Terrace of Opa restaurant, 14 North Parade, BA2 4AJ
opabath.com

Beside the River Avon, on a terrace outside the Opa restaurant, is an ancient-looking alcove with a bench. This is Delia's Grotto, forever associated with an 18th-century scandal. The origins of the grotto are obscure, as is the name (no one seems to have any idea who Delia might have been). However, it is probably not as old as it looks.

The grotto is thought to have been built around 1734 as part of a riverside path and pleasure ground known as 'Harrison's Walk'. This was a popular spot for fashionable visitors to promenade beside the water.

Two regular visitors to the grotto were Richard Brinsley Sheridan and Elizabeth Linley, daughter of the city's Master of Music. Sheridan was an ambitious Irish playwright while Eliza was a talented singer who was sought after by many men. She was once described as 'the most beautiful flower that ever grew in Nature's garden'.

Their relationship was a scandalous affair. The couple attempted to elope to Paris and Sheridan later fought two duels with Thomas Mathews, an army captain who relentlessly pursued Eliza despite the fact that he was already married. The elopement was unsuccessful: Eliza's father brought her back from France and tried to keep the lovers apart.

The hapless couple resorted to leaving letters for one another in Delia's Grotto and eventually – after Eliza dramatically threatened suicide – her father agreed to their marriage in 1773. The union seems to have been rather tempestuous but Sheridan is reported to have been broken-hearted when Eliza died at the age of 38 in 1792.

Their early courtship at the grotto must have made a great impression on Sheridan because he devoted a whole poem to it, with the opening lines, 'Uncouth is this moss-cover'd grotto of stone, And damp is the shade of this dew-dropping tree.'

Delia's Grotto is visible from North Parade Bridge. And on a warm day you can sit beside it on the terrace of the Opa restaurant.

> The Linley family lived at No. 11 Royal Crescent. A plaque outside the house reads: 'Thomas Linley lived here and from this house his daughter Elizabeth eloped with Richard Brinsley Sheridan on the evening of the 18th March 1772.'

Literary Bath

Richard Brinsley Sheridan only lived in Bath for two years, but that was long enough to cause a scandal and for him to write his play *The Rivals*, which was set in the city. There is a plaque to him outside his home on New King Street.

But Sheridan was only one of many writers who lived in Bath and wrote about the city. By the 18th century, it had become a centre of fashionable society and many major literary figures were inspired to visit or make their homes here.

The writer whose name is most associated with Bath is Jane Austen, who lived here between 1801 and 1806 and was a frequent visitor at other times. It seems that her visits were a matter of family duty rather than pleasure, because she is said to have disliked the place. However, that did not stop her from mentioning Bath in every one of her novels.

As you walk around the Georgian city, you are entering the world of Austen's characters. Even those who stayed in more humble dwellings would have been familiar with the grand houses of the Royal Crescent and The Circus; they would have walked from the Upper Town to the shops and other attractions that had sprung up to cater for the new, wealthy residents.

The Pump Room and the Assembly Rooms, both centres of Bath social life at the time, feature in Austen's novels *Persuasion* and *Northanger Abbey*. *Persuasion* also mentions Gravel Walk (see p. 84). You can find out more about the author and her association with Bath at the Jane Austen Centre on Gay Street.

Henry Fielding lived in Bath for a while and he wrote his comic novel *Tom Jones* here in 1749. He often visited Ralph Allen at his home in Prior Park and modelled the character of Squire Allworthy on him.

Another friend of Allen's was the London-based poet Alexander Pope, who was a frequent visitor to Bath (Pope's Walk – see p. 304 – was named after him). As well as being a poet, he was very interested in garden design and helped with the layout of the gardens at Prior Park. The grotto in the garden was entirely his own design.

The novelist and playwright Fanny Burney spent some time in the city and is buried at St Swithin's Church. And the eccentric William Beckford (see p. 164) lived here for many years. Other notable literary visitors of the time include Samuel Johnson and Horace Walpole.

A near contemporary of Jane Austen, but a very different kind of writer, was Mary Shelley. Between 1816 and 1817 she lived in Abbey Courtyard in Bath and it was here that she wrote much of her classic novel *Frankenstein*. That legacy is now explored at Mary Shelley's House of Frankenstein, a multi-sensory museum and escape room on Gay Street.

Bath ceased to be quite so fashionable in the later 19th century. However, one notable visitor was Charles Dickens. He often stayed with his friend Walter Savage Landor in St James's Square or at the York House Hotel on George Street. He may also have stayed at the Saracen's Head on Broad Street (probably the oldest pub in Bath). Bath features in Dickens' novel *The Pickwick Papers* and it is said that Moses Pickwick, the protagonist, was based on the landlord of the White Hart Inn (unfortunately no longer standing). His servant Sam Weller is said to have drunk in what is now the Sam Weller's pub on Upper Borough Walls. It is also claimed that a shop in St James's Square (now a private home) was the inspiration for *The Old Curiosity Shop*.

Moving forward to the 20th century, Georgette Heyer set many of her Regency romances in Bath. Angela Carter, author of many novels including *Nights at The Circus*, lived here during the 1970s. Finally there is John Betjeman, who was Poet Laureate from 1972 to 1984. But his association with Bath is not primarily literary. He was very concerned with the preservation of the architectural heritage and was a trustee of the Bath Preservation Trust. His 1973 poem 'The Sack of Bath' was a critical response to the demolition of Southgate and the modern buildings that replaced it.

Hopefully Betjeman would have been reassured by more recent efforts to maintain the city's Georgian heritage and the designation of Bath as a World Heritage Site in 1987 (see p. 36). And he would surely have approved of the current flourishing of literary pursuits in the annual Bath Festival.

THE MONK'S MILL

A small remnant of medieval Bath

Parade Gardens, Grand Parade, BA2 4DF
Daily 10am–6pm
Small entrance charge (free to local residents with Discovery Card)

Among the formal plantings and sculptures of the Parade Gardens is what appears to be a rather neglected fragment of masonry. This is the Monk's Mill, a rare medieval survival in the centre of Bath and a clue as to how the town might once have looked.

The land on which the Parade Gardens were built lay outside the city wall and was once part of an orchard belonging to the Abbey. A mill on the site is recorded in the Domesday Book but this earlier structure was probably replaced by the Monk's Mill in the 13th century.

The mill was accessed from the town via the East Gate (see p. 66). It was used to clean and process wool for use by the monks. As for most of Bath in the Middle Ages, woollen cloth was central to the abbey's economy.

Although the current Pulteney Weir was built in the 1970s, the River Avon has been dammed since Saxon times. This created a difference in the water level that could be used to drive a waterwheel. Unfortunately it also had the side effect of limiting navigation on the river. This was an ongoing source of friction between the mill owners and other traders who relied upon river transport.

In the Middle Ages the weir ran diagonally across the river, enabling two mills to operate, one on either side of the river. The Bathwick Mill, on the opposite bank, has now disappeared.

Only a fragment of the Monk's Mill remains, surrounded by a small area of ornamental plants. However, there is one curiosity to be spotted. A carved block on the side of the stone appears to show crossed keys, the symbol of St Peter. Did this bit of recycling come from the abbey buildings or was it added deliberately to emphasise that the church owned the mill?

As you walk around the Parade Gardens have a look at the statues and other features, such as the bandstand and the colonnades. At the entrance you pass a bronze statue of the angel of peace, a memorial to King Edward VII. And inside the gardens are a statue of Mozart and another of Bladud, the legendary founder of Bath, together with his pigs.

Bladud, the legendary founder of Bath: why is he associated with pigs?

The statue of King Bladud in Parade Gardens was carved by Stefano Valerio Pieroni in 1859 and originally stood on top of a drinking fountain in Bath Street. It was later removed and had a variety of homes before moving to its current location in 2008. A pig, created by Nigel Bryant and students from Bath College, was added the following year. But who was King Bladud and why is he associated with pigs? Different versions of the legend exist but they all agree that Bladud was the original founder of the city of Bath. The first written mention comes in Geoffrey of Monmouth's semi-fictional *History of the Kings of Britain*, written around 1136. In this version of the story Bladud, the son of King Hudibras, was a necromancer who created hot springs with mystical properties and founded a city (Bath) around them. These springs were supposedly dedicated to the goddess Minerva, although as Bladud lived in the 9th century BCE, long before the Roman invasion of Britain, this part of the story seems rather unlikely. Geoffrey of Monmouth goes on to say that Bladud died when he built a pair of wings, attempted to fly and came crashing to the ground, and that he was the father of King Lear, later immortalised by Shakespeare. But there is no mention of pigs in his account. In fact, it isn't clear when the pigs came into the story. Like all good legends, the tale of Bladud was embellished over time. And it is likely that Christian commentators were keen to establish a more 'rational' explanation for the discovery of Bath's hot springs than attributing them to the work of a sorcerer. According to the story that we know today, in 863 BCE Bladud, then a prince of the Britons, went to study in Athens. While there, he contracted leprosy and found himself shunned when he returned home. He adopted the disguise of a swineherd and took to roaming the country with a herd of pigs. Approaching the River Avon, Bladud stopped to allow his pigs to roll in the mud. When they emerged, he was astounded to note that the animals – who also suffered from leprosy – were completely clear of their spots. Curious, he stepped into the mud himself and was delighted to find himself cured. Bladud was now able to reclaim his kingdom but first he founded a new city around the miraculous healing waters. He dedicated the town to Sul (or Sulis), who later gave her name to the Roman Aquae Sulis. Whatever the truth of the legend, Bladud has become embedded in the local landscape. Both Swineford, on the banks of the Avon close to Saltford, and Swainswick, to the east of the city, claim to take their name from his pigs (or 'swine'). And local legend says that Twerton Roundhill, once (wrongly) thought to be an artificial burial mound, is where Bladud was finally buried. Of course, there are lots of visual reminders of Bath's founder. Apart from the sculpture in Parade Gardens, you'll find an older statue in the King's Bath (see p. 32). Bladud also features in the carved stone frieze above the Podium (see p. 102) and his name lives on in Bladud's Buildings on the Paragon and at the Bladud's Head pub in Swainswick. If you want to know more, have a look at the small display of information and images of Bladud in the Roman Baths, beside the Pump Room.

'WATER IS BEST' INSCRIPTION

A healthy alternative to alcohol in a city that had a problem with drunkenness

Statue of Rebecca at the well
North side of Bath Abbey, BA1 1LT

Hordes of tourists rush past the statue of Rebecca on their way to the abbey every day, but few stop to look closely or to wonder why she is there. Yet there is more to the life-sized figure of a woman pouring water from a jug than is obvious at first glance.

Perhaps the inscription at the base – which reads 'Water is Best' – is a clue? After all, the same phrase (albeit in ancient Greek) appears on the facade of the nearby Pump Room. It is a quote from the poet Pindar and can be seen as a reference to the hot thermal waters that have been a part of the city's history since Roman times.

In Rebecca's case, however, the quotation is a different sort of clue, reinforced by a further inscription at the back of the statue, stating that it was erected by the Bath Temperance Association in 1861.

In the mid-19th century, like many other cities, Bath had a problem with drunkenness. This was partly because there was no safe water supply and beverages such as tea and coffee were too expensive for most people. So people of all ages would drink beer – and stronger tipples such as gin – on a regular basis throughout the day.

In the centre of Bath, the problem was compounded by the presence of several pubs on the High Street near the abbey, and of queues of cab drivers waiting for custom in the adjacent Orange Grove.

The eminently practical solution adopted by Temperance Societies across the country was to erect water fountains to provide a healthy alternative to alcohol. The fountain outside Bath Abbey drew on a biblical theme, with a sculpture of Rebecca, the wife of Isaac, drawing water from a well.

Whether cab drivers and others were persuaded out of the pubs, and whether they concurred that 'water is best', is not recorded! However, it is a fact that the number of pubs in this area – and across the city – gradually declined and that all the notorious institutions in the High Street disappeared.

The fountain carried on dispensing water until the 1980s, when it was renovated. The small bronze angel in a niche beneath the statue was added at this time.

GUILDHALL
BANQUETING ROOM

Bath's finest Georgian interior

Guildhall, High Street, BA1 5AW
Open for concerts and other events throughout the year

In the 18th century, Bath was one of the most fashionable cities in England. It was full of ballrooms and other venues where wealthy people could meet, be entertained and search for husbands for their daughters. One of the grandest, and most important, of these places was the Guildhall Banqueting Room, now hidden away in a civic building.

The current Guildhall is the third on the present site and was built by Thomas Baldwin in the 1770s. Although it was designed primarily as a municipal building, it seems that no expense was spared as all the rooms are richly decorated. The Council Chamber is particularly ornate, perhaps a reflection of the fact that in the 18th century members of the council tended to be the city's most influential citizens.

The most opulent space was the Banqueting Room, said to be Bath's finest Georgian interior. This is where the city's most prominent citizens and visitors would have mingled. It is the sort of place where you could imagine Jane Austen – and her fictional heroines – meeting potential suitors and gossiping with their friends.

This vast room features Corinthian columns, ornate gilding and a musicians' gallery. Around the walls are oil paintings of notable Bath citizens. These include Ralph Allen (see p. 280) and Field Marshal George Wade, an eminent military man and MP for Bath.

As you walk into the Banqueting Room, your eye is immediately drawn to the three massive crystal chandeliers. These were handmade by William Parker in 1778. Each chandelier is said to take a whole day to clean, a laborious process that involves lowering it to the floor and then very carefully taking it apart!

Today the Guildhall is primarily used as council offices and as the home of the City Archives. And the city's councillors still have a grand chamber in which to conduct their business. However, the Banqueting Room is in great demand for weddings and other private functions. It has also been used as a film location – most recently in the popular TV series, *Bridgerton*.

If you don't have the good fortune to be invited to a wedding in the Guildhall, the best way to see the Banqueting Room is to attend one of the concerts or other performances that are hosted here. You'll find several opportunities to visit during the annual Bath Festival in May and at other events throughout the year.

PILLAR IN GUILDHALL MARKET

Paying on the nail

Guildhall Market, High Street, BA2 4AW
The pillar is close to the High Street entrance
Market: Mon–Sat 9am–5am

The phrase 'to pay on the nail' refers to full and prompt payment of an amount owing. But where did the phrase come from? If a notice in the Guildhall Market is to be believed, the answer lies in an 18th-century pillar close to the entrance.

A notice above this squat stone pillar states that: 'This eighteenth century pillar or "nail" stood on the site of the present markets in 1768 for the transaction of business and for prompt payment in bargaining. It is said that this gave origin to the phrase "on the nail".' But while there is no reason to doubt that payments were settled on the nail, is this really the origin of the phrase?

The first thing to note is that the Bath nail is not the only one to make this claim. In the nearby city of Bristol, you can see three nails that are also said to have given rise to the phrase. Not only are these nails considerably larger, but they are also rather older, the oldest going back to the 1550s. And similar nails are to be found in Liverpool and Limerick.

More confusing still, some people maintain that the phrase pre-dates all these pillars. Linguistic experts point out that the Anglo-French phrase *payer sur le ungle* was in use in the 14th century, referring to a fingernail and suggesting the idea of counting out money with the fingertips.

Whatever the truth of the story, the pillar does remind us of the lost traditions of a market that has been in existence for around 800 years. The medieval market cross, the stocks and the pillory have now all disappeared, as have the mess and the smells that would once have surrounded the stalls.

But sharp-eyed visitors will find one other reminder of past times. If you exit the market by the back entrance you'll see an extract from the 1864 by-laws, including the exhortation that 'no person shall throw or fling vegetables, garbage or any missile in the market'!

THE EAST GATE

A medieval gateway into the city

Boat Stall Lane, BA2 4AN (behind the Guildhall)

Back in the days when Bath was a walled city (see p. 16), there were four entrances (or 'gates') into the town. Three of these have now disappeared but, if you look hard enough, you can still see the old East Gate.

The gate is not immediately obvious, visible only from a car park behind the Guildhall and the market. When you do locate it, you'll notice that it's a long way beneath ground level. This is because the street level was artificially raised during the 18th century to avoid flooding, leaving much of the medieval city underground.

The East Gate was the smallest of the city gates and the only one that wasn't locked at night. The other gates led to major routes out of the city and had to accommodate horses and carriages as well as large groups of people. The East Gate, on the other hand, was close to the river, with a narrow path between the gate and the water.

Although you can no longer walk through the gate (access is restricted to council employees), you can look down Boat Stall Lane, the short street that would once have been followed by people leaving the city via the East Gate. This would take them to the river, or to Monk's Mill, the remains of which can now be seen in Parade Gardens (see p. 56).

If you cross the river via Pulteney Bridge and stand on the opposite bank, you can see the opening where Boat Stall Lane joined the river. From here, people could take a ferry across to the other side or join a boat that was travelling downstream to the sea.

The local stone was too soft to be suitable for fortifications

A particular item of interest is that – like other remnants of the city walls – the East Gate is not built from the local Bath stone. The darker – and harder – stone had to be brought into the city to build the walls as the local stone was too soft to be suitable for fortifications.

ART STORE TOURS

Discover hidden artworks

Victoria Art Gallery, Bridge Street, BA2 4AT
01225 477233
victoriagal.org.uk/event/art-store-tours
Free monthly tours: 12–12.45pm
See website for dates: essential to book in advance

L ike many galleries and museums, the Victoria Art Gallery has far more artworks than it has room to display. The free monthly art tours are an opportunity to explore some hidden treasures, learn more about the collections and discover a few curiosities that are rarely on show.

The gallery was designed to commemorate Queen Victoria's 60 years on the throne and opened to the public in 1900. Through a mixture of purchases and donations it now holds around 14,000 artworks, both paintings and decorative items. However, only around 1,500 can be displayed at any one time.

Exhibits are rotated as often as possible and some are kept in 'open storage', in glass cases in the museum itself. But some items rarely, if ever, see the light of day and you need to descend to the basement to see them. The basement has a history of its own. Backing onto the river and Pulteney Weir, it was once used as an abattoir and later became the

stables of a nearby hotel. But now it is an air-conditioned space packed full of hidden art.

What you see on a tour varies from one time to another. However, you are sure to be shown round by a knowledgeable curator and to view a wide variety of artworks. Tours begin with the decorative arts room, which is full of cupboards with items such as Delftware, glass and household objects. Some pieces are chipped or broken and not suitable for display. Others are what one guide describes as 'whacky stuff': a random selection of mismatched china, bizarre ornaments and items whose purpose can only be guessed at.

Then there is the watercolour room (full of pictures, sketches and lithographs as well as some original lithograph blocks) and the oil painting room. The latter has pictures by Walter Sickert and Joshua Reynolds as well as works by much lesser-known artists, all arranged on pull-out screens.

A bonus of the tour is that visitors are allowed to open cupboards and pull out screens to get a good look at items that are normally hidden.

Upper Town

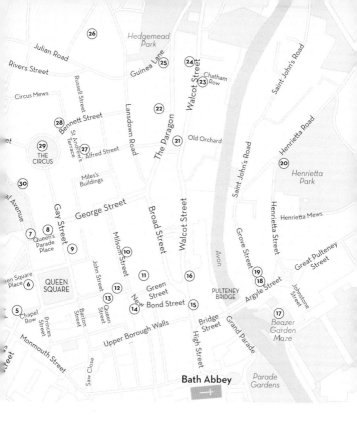

STOTHERT & PITT STEAM CRANE

A relic of Bath's industrial past

Victoria Bridge Road, BA2 3EB

The factories and workshops on the western side of Bath have gradually given way to housing but you will find occasional reminders of the city's industrial past. One example is the Stothert & Pitt steam crane that stands, seemingly incongruously, beside the modern homes of the Western Riverside development.

Founded in Bath in 1855, the engineering company Stothert & Pitt became the city's largest employer until it closed in 1989. The firm manufactured all sorts of iron structures, including railway engines and river bridges. However, they were best known for their cranes, initially used in the local stone quarries but later exported worldwide.

After the business closed, its main site was redeveloped for housing and leisure. The developers were keen to recognise the site's heritage and worked with Bryan Chalker, a one-time mayor of Bath, to rescue a crane that was lying abandoned in the Washford railway goods yard in Minehead.

This was a rail-mounted, self-propelled steam crane built in 1904. Crane No. 312 – as it was known – was not built to an existing pattern but assembled from parts for the factory's own use. This gave it a unique place in the company's history.

Moving the crane back to its original home was a major challenge: at around 5 metres high and weighing 34 tonnes, it took 9 hours to travel the 110 km from Minehead to Bath. Once in place, the long work of restoration and repainting began.

It seems that there was some debate over the restoration. No. 312 had seen some changes over its working life, and sides had been added to the cab (which was originally just a roof) in the 1920s. The later version seems to have triumphed and the extended cab has been retained – what you see now is a crane that looks ready and waiting to spring into action.

Newark Works

If you walk along the river towards the railway station, you'll come to a second Stothert & Pitt site: the Newark Works. This has now been repurposed as a co-working space and in 2023 another crane was placed outside. This one was built in 1864 and is the oldest Stothert & Pitt crane to have survived intact.

VICTORIA BRIDGE

The best surviving example of a Dredge taper bridge

Victoria Bridge Road, BA2 3FQ

As a pedestrian footbridge outside the city centre, the Victoria Bridge is one of the River Avon's lesser-known crossings. And those who do walk across it may be unaware that they are experiencing a marvel of civil engineering and a piece of Bath's industrial history.

Built in 1836, the Victoria Bridge is the earliest example of a Dredge taper bridge designed by James Dredge, a Bath-based brewer. He seems to have had an interest in bridges, having bid – unsuccessfully – to design the Bristol Suspension Bridge, but he may also have had solid commercial reasons for a more local bridge.

At that time, moving beer across the river from his brewery on the Lower Bristol Road would have necessitated either a long detour or a ferry crossing. And, of course, the fact that he could charge a toll to other traders using the bridge may also have been a consideration.

The design of the new bridge was revolutionary. Unlike other suspension bridges of the time, the Victoria Bridge was a sort of double cantilever, using angled chains rather than the more usual vertical supports. This became the prototype for several other bridges in the UK and elsewhere, but the Victoria Bridge is the best surviving example.

Despite its historical significance, the Victoria Bridge was almost lost when it closed in 2010 due to safety concerns. However, it was later rebuilt as part of the regeneration of the riverside area, using as much of the original structure and fabric as possible.

Today those crossing the bridge are walkers and cyclists rather than horses and carts. And they are more likely to be going to the new residential developments than to the now-disappeared factories and warehouses. But the Victoria Bridge remains as a monument to Bath's industrial past.

Industrial heritage in Elizabeth Park

Close by is Elizabeth Park, which is home to several specially commissioned sculptures, including the dramatic *Maid of the Park*, fashioned from pieces of ironwork left over from the Victoria Bridge renovation. Look out for two of the ornamental ends from the old Destructor Bridge – a former railway crossing – that have been salvaged and painted bright blue and orange!

WATCHMAN'S BOX
ON NORFOLK CRESCENT

An early form of crime prevention

Norfolk Crescent, BA1 2BE

Despite the genteel image of Georgian Bath, the influx of wealth into a formerly impoverished city provided new opportunities for crime in the 18th and 19th centuries. The problem was made worse by the fact that the existence of theatres, assembly rooms and other entertainments meant that rich incomers would often return to their homes late at night.

Prior to the 1830s there was no organised police force and residents were obliged to organise their own protection. The solution was often to employ a night watchman whose job was to patrol the street during the hours of darkness and to stop anyone thought to be acting suspiciously.

Watchman's boxes had the dual function of shelter for the watchman and – if necessary – providing a convenient lock-up for miscreants. As they were often built of timber, most have now disappeared, but a rare survivor from this period is the box on Norfolk Crescent. This is one of Bath's lesser-known crescents, built by John Palmer at the beginning of the 19th century.

Palmer is also thought to have designed the watchman's hut. This is a functional circular structure built from limestone with a wooden door but embellishments such as a frieze around the top. Today you can look at the box from the outside, standing at the edge of the open space that was once the garden of the crescent.

A sign above the door reads: 'This the only remaining City Watchman's Sentry Box in Bath, was restored by the Urban Sanitary Authority in 1836. Any person found damaging the same or trespassing therein will be prosecuted.'

The Norfolk Crescent box is not the only remaining sentry box in Bath. In 1840 two stone watchman's boxes were built outside the Sydney Hotel (now the Holburne Museum). They are still there, on the street outside the museum. However, they provided shelter only and were not lock-ups.

TELESCOPE PLATFORM
AT THE HERSCHEL MUSEUM

Marking the place where Uranus was first discovered

Herschel Museum of Astronomy, 19 New King Street, BA1 2BL
herschelmuseum.org.uk
11 Feb–31 Dec (exc. 25 and 26 Dec): Tues–Sun, 10am–5pm (closed 1pm–2pm
at weekends). Last entry 4pm

In 1781 the astronomer William Herschel discovered the planet Uranus from the garden of his home in Bath. And in 2022 a memorial was placed at the spot where his telescope had stood. Its function is not purely commemorative: it is also used as a platform for astronomical viewing sessions.

Herschel was a professional musician who moved to Bath from Germany in 1766. Together with his sister Caroline, who acted as his housekeeper, he developed a passion for astronomy. He began to design and build his own telescopes and use them to observe the sky. Between them, William and Caroline discovered 2,400 new astronomical objects, including stars, nebulae and comets.

But it is the discovery of Uranus for which William is best known. This was the first planet to be discovered using a telescope: previously known planets were all visible to the naked eye. The discovery was also significant in that it doubled the known size of the solar system.

The house in which the Herschels lived was purchased and turned into a museum in 1981. And in 2022, 200 years after William's death, the Bath Preservation Trust erected a memorial at the exact place where Uranus had been discovered. Created by Iain Cotton, this took the form of a stone platform built from Forest of Dean blue sandstone, which has a similar colour to that of Uranus.

At the centre of the stone is a reflective stainless steel disc. This is the same size as the metal mirrors in the telescope that William was using when he first spotted Uranus. It is now used as a platform for star-gazing sessions, both solar and night-time. And in a reminder of the history of the house and its garden, these sessions sometimes use replicas of William's own telescopes.

'He broke through the confines of the heavens'

There are several other items of interest in the garden, including a sculpture of William and Caroline, a metal sculpture representing Uranus and a granite plaque with a plan of the solar system.

At the back of the garden is an orrery (a mechanical model of the solar system) and behind this is a plaque in the ground. The plaque was originally in Westminster Abbey but was later gifted to the museum. Around the edge is a quotation in Latin, part of which translates as 'He broke through the confines of the heavens.'

TEMPLE ORNAMENT

A folly on the site of a demolished chapel

Chapel Row, BA1 1HN

Beside Holy Trinity Church on Chapel Row, you'll see a curious monument amongst the foliage. Is it a miniature temple or a Georgian folly? Or is it a 20th-century assemblage, created from the ruins of an old chapel?

The Temple Ornament stands on the site of the former St Mary's Chapel, built by John Wood the Elder in the 1730s. This was the earliest proprietary chapel in Bath, designed for wealthy residents to worship in private without rubbing shoulders with the hoi polloi. By all accounts it was a fine building, modelled on a church by Inigo Jones in London's Covent Garden.

Unfortunately the chapel was demolished some time around 1875, when the road was widened to improve access to the nearby Green Park railway station. Fragments of the building were taken away to adorn private properties elsewhere in the city (you'll still see a Greek-style column and other remnants if you stand at the end of Cleveland Bridge and peer into the garden of No. 4 Cleveland Place West).

Apart from the trees that surround it, the Temple Ornament is all that stands on the site of the former chapel. Its origins are obscure, but we know that in 1976 it was rescued from the garden of a house on Queen Square, where it had fallen into disrepair. It was restored by students from Bath College and moved to its present location.

It is generally thought that the ornament was constructed from bits of the demolished chapel; an alternative theory is that its components came from the Queen's Bath. Either way, with its Ionic columns and symmetrical design, it manages to resemble a small, but perfectly formed, classical temple.

CEILING PAINTINGS BY ANDREA CASALI

Ornate paintings in the museum's meeting room

Bath Royal Literary and Scientific Institution
16–18 Queen Square, BA1 2HN
01225 312084
brlsi.org
Mon–Sat 10am–4pm; also evening events

The Bath Royal Literary and Scientific Institution (known as the BRLSI) is a small but fascinating museum on Queen Square. It is full of varied and sometimes unexpected exhibits, including some that are not on general display. These include the Casali ceiling paintings in one of the upstairs meeting rooms.

Established in 1825, the BRLSI is the nearest that Bath has to a general museum covering a range of subjects. Originally housed in Terrace Walk, it moved to its current home in 1932. It was once the house of Dr William Oliver, who founded the Royal Mineral Hospital in Bath and is known as the inventor of the famous Bath Oliver biscuit.

The four paintings by Andrea Casali were purchased for the BRLSI by Hastings Elwin in 1923. Painted in the 1750s, they were originally commissioned by Alderman Beckford for his mansion at Fonthill Splendens in Wiltshire. They were subsequently sold by his son William (see p. 164) and eventually found their way to the ceiling of what is now known as the Elwin Room.

Casali was an Italian painter and art dealer who spent much of his life in England. He was known for his large mythological and allegorical paintings. The ones in the Elwin Room represent Roman gods: Ceres, goddess of plants; Mercury, god of trade and commerce; Faunus, god of woods and fields; and Pomona, goddess of fruit and orchards.

Today the Elwin Room is used for a variety of public meetings and events in the evenings. If it is not in use, you may also be able to see the paintings during daytime opening hours: inquire in advance or ask at the reception desk.

Exhibitions at the BRLSI change regularly but you may be surprised by some of the items on permanent display. In the meeting room adjacent to the Elwin Room is a rare cast of a complete skeleton of the pliosaur *Rhomaleosaurus cramptoni*. And in the main museum area is the original manuscript of Charles Darwin's book, *On the Origin of Species*.

GRAVEL WALK

An 18th-century lovers' lane

Victoria Park
Runs from Queen's Parade Place to Brock Street, BA1 2NN

In Regency times, the busy roads of Brock Street and Gay Street were full of carriages and horses, throwing up dust and mud. Ladies walking to or from the Pump Room, the shops or the Assembly Rooms would struggle to keep their shoes and dresses clean. Worse still, they were exposed to the public gaze: this was not the place for a private conversation with an intimate friend or a potential suitor.

Gravel Walk was created in 1771 as a pedestrian path bypassing the traffic. It was a secluded walk, passing the gardens at the back of The Circus and Gay Street. Then, as now, it must have had the feeling of a country stroll, bordered by trees and open parkland.

It soon became known as a sort of lovers' lane, a place where courting couples could find a modicum of privacy. A famous contemporary account can be found in Jane Austen's novel *Persuasion*, where we see Anne Elliot and Captain Wentworth conducting an important conversation while following 'the comparatively quiet and retired gravel walk'.

Perhaps surprisingly, Gravel Walk remains quiet and secluded today. Just as in the 18th century, it is an oasis of calm between the bustle of the city and the activity of Victoria Park.

One of the city's duelling grounds

Although the path was peaceful when ladies were out walking, it was sometimes a bit livelier early in the morning. One of the city's duelling grounds was beside Gravel Walk, and the dawn air would occasionally ring with the sounds of guns or swords and screams. All that remains now of the duelling ground is a large depression in the earth covered with trees and bushes and – reputedly – frequented by the spirits of duellers who met their end here.

If you pass through at night, watch out for ghosts …

SEDAN-CHAIR HOUSES

Where chair-carriers waited for their fares

Queen's Parade Place, BA1 2NN

Queen's Parade Place is a quiet street and passers-by don't always stop to look at the pair of tiny but perfectly formed buildings in an otherwise undistinguished row. These are the only purpose-built sedan-chair houses to be found in Britain.

Sedan chairs became popular in the mid-17th century. A single chair was encased in a wooden box with long poles attached so that two carriers – one at the front and one at the back – could carry the chair and its occupant to wherever they wished to go.

Although they weren't very comfortable, sedan chairs were often favoured over horse-drawn hackney cabs in Bath, partly because they were cheaper and partly because they were better suited to the city's steep hills and narrow lanes.

However, the carriers had a reputation for being rude and less than attentive to their customers. It was left to Beau Nash, the 18th-century Master of Ceremonies for Bath, to license the chairmen, regulate their behaviour and set fixed fares for their journeys.

The sedan-chair houses were built to give the chairmen somewhere to rest or wait between fares. They were equipped with fires, a facility that must have been appreciated by carriers who became cold and wet as they traipsed from one house to another.

The houses might have been plain inside but the exteriors were carefully designed by John Wood. Not only were they perfectly proportioned, but each house had a curved wall attached to the front, intended to suggest the shape of a sedan chair.

Today the right-hand house is the head office of Hawker Joinery, a bespoke heritage joinery that has worked on many of Bath's listed buildings. They have renovated the building with ornate woodwork that would not have been out of place in a much grander Georgian setting. Although it is not open to the public, if the door is open, you can peek inside to see an interior that John Wood himself would surely have admired. And in the corner, you can still see the fireplace where sedan chairmen once kept themselves warm.

The sedan chair outside the house is also the work of Hawker Joinery, as is a similar chair outside the museum at No. 1 Royal Crescent. A reminder of a time when travel was less comfortable than it is today!

GEORGIAN WIG-POWDERING ROOM

Where gentlemen powdered their wigs

41 Gay Street, BA1 2NT
Visible through the window 24/7

If you peer through the window of the building on the corner of Gay Street and Old King Street, you'll see a small triangular room with an ornate tiled niche and marble basin. Sadly it is no longer in use, but it is a rare surviving example of an important feature of any Georgian house: a wig-powdering room.

Although it now serves as the Bath office of Morgan Financial, the interior of the house at No. 41 Gay Street is still laid out much as it was when it was built in the 1730s. This includes a room whose sole purpose was the powdering of gentlemen's wigs.

Wigs for men were very fashionable at the beginning of the 18th century but they seem to have required a certain amount of maintenance. They were long and curly and were often slicked down with a greasy pomade made from lard or other fats. As a result, they tended to become rather dirty and smelly. It was also considered desirable for wigs to be as white as possible. The solution was to cover them with powder at frequent intervals as a way of whitening the hair and absorbing the odours.

Through the window of the Gay Street house, you'll spot a hole in the basin which once held a head-shaped stand to place the wigs on while they were being powdered. It was a very messy business and presumably left lots of grease and dust for the servants to clean up.

The room may have been functional but it was also ornate. Apart from the marble basin and surround, the curved wall of the closet is lined with blue Delft tiles and topped by a carved scallop niche.

Perhaps fortunately for everyone, gentlemen's wigs eventually fell out of fashion and powder rooms were no longer required. But the Gay Street room remains as a curiosity from the past.

Who lived at No. 41 Gay Street?

A plaque on the outside wall of the house says that this was once the home of John Wood the Younger. However, although Wood was certainly the architect, it is doubtful whether he actually lived here: records show that the first occupant was Richard Marchant, a wealthy Quaker.

JOLLY'S HERITAGE ROOM

*Discover the history of one of Europe's oldest
department stores*

*House of Fraser, 13 Milsom Street, BA1 1DD
Mon–Fri 10am–6pm, Sat 9am–6pm, Sun 11am–5pm*

Jolly's on Milsom street is one of the oldest, and grandest, department stores in Europe. It has a long and fascinating history and the building has retained many of its ornamental features. Visitors can learn more about the shop, and its place in the city's history, in a small heritage room crammed full of interesting artefacts.

James Jolly opened his first shop in Bath (having previously traded in Kent) in 1823. The city had become very fashionable, attracting visitors with money to spend, and in 1831 Jolly and his son Thomas opened the 'Bath Emporium' on Milsom Street, selling a range of household, luxury and novelty goods.

The shop gradually expanded to take over neighbouring buildings on Milsom Street. Over the years it was patronised by many eminent customers, including Queen Mary, wife of George V, who became a regular shopper here.

Jolly's remained a family business until it was sold in 1970. It is now owned by House of Fraser but it still has the feel of a stately, upmarket emporium. It is clearly proud of its history, and a series of heritage plaques around the store tell the story of the business and its customers.

You can find the heritage room at the top of the stairs behind the Flannels department. It has a range of artefacts covering the period during which the shop has traded. There are shelves lined with books, and display cases with letters, photos and sale notices. Old labels give an idea of the range of goods sold and the prices charged.

On the walls are pictures and artefacts, including Queen Victoria's mourning silk. There is even an old clocking-in machine of the type once routinely used to monitor the comings and goings of staff. It all goes to build up a picture of the social life of Bath over the last 200 years and the role of its first department store.

As you walk around the store look for the original decorative items, including fireplaces and elaborately carved cornices and mouldings. Perhaps the best-known feature is the peacock motif on the ground floor, an art nouveau mosaic created in the 1900s.

OCTAGON CHAPEL

A once-fashionable place of worship

*Botanist Bar and Restaurant, part 46A Milsom Place and 28 Milsom Street,
BA1 1BZ*
thebotanist.uk.com/locations/bath
*Mon–Wed noon–11pm, Thurs and Fri noon–midnight, Sat 10am–1am,
Sun 10am–11pm*

On the edge of the Milsom Court shopping area, and entered via a covered passage, the Botanist restaurant appears hidden from the outside world. It's not until you get inside that you realise you are in what was one of Bath's most fashionable 18th-century chapels.

The Octagon was built by Timothy Lightoler in 1767. Even at that time, its splendour was within rather than without, as it was encased within blank windowless walls. But the interior was an elegant octagon, a shape favoured by preachers of the time as it enabled members of the congregation to sit close to the pulpit.

This was a privately owned proprietary chapel. This meant that it did not need to be consecrated and was free to invite visiting preachers of different denominations. It seems that the Octagon was a fashionable meeting place from the outset. People paid for their pews, the most expensive of which were in fact small recesses, complete with fireplaces and easy chairs. Accounts exist of footmen stoking up the fires before the sermon began.

The Octagon remained as a chapel until 1895. Since then it has been used for a variety of purposes, including an antiques showroom and the headquarters of the Royal Photographic Society. It has been home to the Botanist restaurant since 2019. Throughout its different uses, the building has retained its octagonal shape and many original features. The restaurant space, the central bar and the upper gallery are all octagonal. The columns and plasterwork remain, as do parts of the recesses and the dome that tops the whole structure.

One part of the original usage remains: the vaults are still full of spirits. But the drinks have changed and they are drunk rather than stored. This is now a trendy cocktail bar, with specialist gins, liqueurs and botanical blends.

It is said that Jane Austen was a regular visitor to the Octagon. The resident organist was William Herschel, the Bath-based astronomer (see p. 78).

'Spirits above and spirits below'

The vaults of the building were used by wealthy residents for a different purpose – the storage of wine. This gave rise to a rhyme with the opening line 'Spirits above and spirits below'.

GRAND EASTERN RESTAURANT ⑫

A hidden Georgian interior

8A Quiet Street, BA1 2JS
01225 422323
grandeastern.co.uk
See website for opening times

From the outside you wouldn't expect the Grand Eastern to be anything other than a conventional Indian restaurant. But climb the stairs and you'll find yourself in a fine Georgian interior, adorned with some contemporary Indian murals.

Although there's not much to attract the attention of passers-by, look closely and you'll see that part of the Georgian exterior remains. Standing on the opposite side of the road, look up to see two statues (representing 'Commerce' and 'Genius') carved in the niches and a statue of Mercury above the pediment. However, these give no clue as to what you will find inside.

The first indication that this may be no ordinary building comes as you walk up the stairs and spot a striking mural of a young woman sitting on the wall of an oriental arcade with columns and arches. But the restaurant itself, with its magnificent setting, is likely to take you by surprise.

Built in 1824, the building on Quiet Street was a mixed-used development, with shops on the ground floor and public rooms upstairs. The Grand Eastern uses part of the upper area, originally the 'Auction Mart & Bazaar', a place for meetings and exhibitions. It later became a Methodist chapel (some sources will tell you that this room was at one time a ballroom, but there seems to be no firm evidence for this).

The structure of the Georgian interior has mostly been retained. The vaulted room is topped by three glass domes, and large windows at either end fill it with natural light. Around the sides are a series of large and colourful murals.

These paintings were added in 2009 when the restaurant was renovated and redesigned. They are the work of Apulpan Ditt, an international artist and a friend of the then owner. He hand painted three

pictures of Moghul life, with sumptuous Indian interiors, courtyards, diners and dancers. The fourth mural – the one at the top of the stairs – was added in 2016.

You can see the restaurant and its murals at any time during opening hours. And you can get a very good Indian meal here too!

SECRET LIBRARY AT THE RAVEN

A library in a pub

The Raven, 7 Queen Street, BA1 1HE
theravenofbath.co.uk
Mon–Thurs 11am–11pm, Fri and Sat 11am–midnight, Sun 11am–10.30pm

The Raven is one of the most historic pubs in Bath. It has always been a place to enjoy a quiet drink (and perhaps a pie as well) in atmospheric surroundings, but now you can relax with a book as well.

In the summer of 2022, The Raven expanded into the upper floors of the building on Queen Street. This means that – like a proper old-fashioned pub – it now has six separate drinking spaces, making it easy to hide yourself away should you wish to do so.

Better still, two of the new bars are themed. Walk up the steps at the back of the upstairs bar and you'll find yourself in The Gallery, its walls covered with pictures. And at the very top of the building is the Secret Library.

The walls of the library are lined with books, apparently donated by a bookseller relative of one of the builders who worked on the redesign project. They are arranged loosely by subject, an eclectic mixture of themes including history, music and graphic novels. There are lots of novels, a small reference section and a collection of children's books (yes, you can bring the younger members of the family with you).

The bar is described as 'Bath's only free lending library in a pub'. As well as sitting and reading the books, customers are encouraged to borrow, swap or donate further titles. So you are likely to find something new every time you visit.

The library also doubles up as an events space where The Raven's regular comedy nights are held. So far, it has also hosted a book launch and a hen night (I am assured that the latter was a very genteel affair!).

The bar in the Secret Library is open on Friday evenings and all day on Saturday and Sunday. But if it's not in use for an event, customers are welcome to take their drinks into the library at any time. A perfect way to while away a rainy afternoon or a long winter's evening.

SCULPTURE OF A CHERUB

All that remains of the Melfort Cross

Junction of Burton Street and Old Bond Street, BA1 1BW

The island block of shops between Burton Street and Old Bond Street is a curiosity in itself, so narrow that the buildings front onto both streets. A detail that might be missed by shoppers hurrying on to Milsom Street is the chubby cherub staring down at them from an alcove at the northern end.

This is all that now remains of the Melfort Cross, which was erected in the Cross Bath in memory of a royal visit. It was at one time fashionable for people of all social classes to come to Bath in search of the healing waters. One such visitor was Mary of Modena, wife of King James II, who visited in 1687 in the hope of conceiving a son.

Her mission was successful and James Stuart was born the following year. Mary was convinced that the thermal waters had aided her fertility, and the Earl of Melfort – a loyal supporter of the king – commissioned a commemorative monument to stand in the Cross Bath. The very ornate Melfort Cross consisted of three columns, a dome and a cross, with three cherubs holding a crown and sceptre.

Unfortunately, King James lost his throne in 1688 and his son James Stuart – who tried to reclaim it – became known as the Old Pretender, leading to almost a century of Jacobite rebellions. So it is perhaps not surprising that the Melfort Cross became a bit of an embarrassment to the city, and a combination of vandalism and civic decree led to its dismantlement.

The remnants of the Melfort Cross were finally removed in 1783, when the Cross Bath was substantially rebuilt. The only bit that remains is a single cherub, rescued by a perfumier who placed it in a niche in the wall of his house at the end of Old Bond Street.

You might be tempted to think that the royal coat of arms above the cherub was a political statement by the perfumier. In fact, this is the coat of arms of Queen Victoria and is a later addition.

SLIPPERY LANE

A hidden medieval street

Northgate Street, BA1 5AS (between Sweaty Betty and New Saville Row)
No access to lane, but visible from the end at any time

Walking down Northgate, it would be easy to miss the entrance to the narrow passage that runs between Sweaty Betty and the New Saville Row barber's shop. But look more closely and you'll get a rare insight into the life of the city in the Middle Ages.

The road in front of you is Slippery Lane, once known as Alford Lane. This narrow cobbled street once ran from the North Gate around the outer edge of the city wall and down to the River Avon. Here a ferry waited to carry passengers across the water (this ferry remained in operation until the construction of Pulteney Bridge in the 18th century).

Although some of the names and routes of Bath's medieval streets remain today (such as Bridewell Lane and Parsonage Lane), these have now become modern thoroughfares. But if you stand at the end of Slippery Lane, you get a real sense of what it might have been like to live in a town where all the roads were narrow, dark and uneven. To get the full picture, however, you also need to envisage the sounds and the smells. The street would have been full of people and dogs, and all sorts of trades were carried on both inside and outside the houses. There were open drains and the road surface would have been covered with refuse and slops (just ask yourself where the 'slippery' name came from …!)

A particular feature of Slippery Lane was the ducking stool that used to stand by the river. This was where people – mostly women, many of them accused of witchcraft – would literally be plunged into the water as a punishment. Sometimes the hapless wretch would drown; if she floated, it was taken as proof that she was in league with the devil.

Unfortunately, the lane is now gated and you can only stand at the end and imagine walking along the ancient street. However, there is an ambitious proposal to redevelop the area and to restore public access to Slippery Lane. Perhaps one day we'll be able to walk in the steps of our medieval ancestors again.

'BATH THROUGH THE AGES' SCULPTURE

A sculpture that few people ever notice

The Podium, Northgate Street, BA1 5AL

Most pedestrians on Northgate Street walk along the wide pavement outside Waitrose and the Central Library. But if you cross to the narrow footpath alongside St Michael's Church, look up to the outside of the Podium. You will see a sculpted frieze that few people ever notice, entitled 'Bath through the Ages'.

Although it is built of Bath stone in a neoclassical style, with columns and arches, the Podium was controversial when it opened at the end of the 1980s. Taking its name from the raised platform above a car park on which it stands, it was built on land previously designated for new law courts and that had been cleared by demolishing a row of 18th-century houses.

This was part of the so-called 'Sack of Bath', in which parts of the city were razed to the ground and rebuilt in a manner unsympathetic to its Georgian heritage. By the time the Podium came to be built, however,

there was more awareness of the need to attempt – even if not always entirely successfully – to blend in with the surroundings.

There was also a growth in the creation of public art during this period. New artworks were particularly associated with cultural buildings, so the Podium, which was to house the library as well as a supermarket, was an obvious candidate for a sculpture (even if it was eventually placed in a position where it would not be visible to many passers-by).

'Bath through the Ages' is a stone relief carved in 1989 by Barry Baldwin, a UK sculptor who has worked on many important buildings including Westminster Abbey and Buckingham Palace. It shows a series of heads, designed to depict the history of Bath from the earliest times to the modern day.

It begins with King Bladud (see p. 58) and moves on to a Roman soldier in front of a Doric column. Then there are Georgian and Victorian heads, with Pulteney Bridge and the Royal Crescent behind them. And, coming right up to date, a busker outside the Pump Room has a policeman lurking beside his shoulder.

Look carefully and you'll see that Bladud is unusually warrior-like, with a leopard's-head hat, and that all sorts of objects are hidden between the heads. The frieze is full of symbolism and deserves more than a passing glance.

BEAZER GARDEN MAZE

A modern labyrinth

Spring Gardens Road, BA2 6PW

Although it sits just beneath the busy Pulteney Bridge, the Beazer Garden Maze seems to be scarcely noticed by passers-by. Children may occasionally run along its paths, and tourists may cast a curious glance as they queue for the popular boat trips along the River Avon. However, few people stop to look at its elaborate mosaics or to wonder about its significance.

The Beazer Garden Maze was created for the 1984 Bath Festival, which had 'the maze' as its theme. It was the work of Randoll Coate, a maze enthusiast with more than 50 labyrinth designs to his name (he was also a diplomat and a wartime spy).

Strictly speaking, this is a labyrinth rather than a maze because it has no dead ends. As is traditional with labyrinths, visitors are invited to follow the path slowly, in a spirit of contemplation. As they approach the centre they are confronted with a series of 'gaze-mazes' – a central mosaic surrounded by six semicircles, concealing different layers of symbolism.

The mosaic itself is made from 92,000 pieces of Italian marble. The central image is a Gorgon's head, representing the sun goddess Minerva Sulis after whom Aquae Sulis, the Roman city of Bath, was named. Around it are pictures of Bladud, the legendary founder of Bath, and of mythological figures representing the city's cultural heritage, framed by the four seasons.

However, the symbolism doesn't stop there. The shape of the maze – an ellipse – was intended to recall the shapes of the nearby Pulteney Weir, of Bath's Victorian railway arches and of the fanlights above the front doors of many Georgian houses.

Taken as a whole, the Beazer Garden Maze portrays the city's Celtic and Roman past, its progress through the centuries and its present. A place to stop and stare, not to rush past.

For more information about the symbolism of labyrinths, see p. 204.

TROMPE-L'ŒIL
OF A MAN READING A BOOK

A deceptive painting

Corner of Argyle Street and Grove Street, BA2 4BA

As you approach Argyle Street from Grove Street, glance up at a first-floor window. You'll see a man in a bookshop, absorbed in reading a book. But peer more closely at his old-fashioned appearance, remind yourself that No. 5 Grove Street is no longer a bookshop and you could be forgiven for thinking you've seen an apparition from the past.

What you're actually looking at is a *trompe-l'œil*, a deceptive painting designed to trick the viewer into imagining that it is real. It was painted onto a blank window by the local firm of Richards and Faulkner in 1994 in recognition of the building's previous existence as a bookshop.

The shop was that of George Gregory, a bookseller, bookbinder and publisher, who traded from here until 1922, when the business was sold to George Bayntun (whose bookshop now trades from premises in Manvers Street).

The *trompe-l'œil* painting depicts the shelves of a bookshop, with a man reading a book called *The 18th Century Architecture of Bath*. Published by George Gregory in 1904, this was a very influential book on Georgian Bath, written by Mowbray A. Green, an architect who worked on various buildings around the city.

The identity of the man in the picture is less certain. Some claim that it is Mowbray Green himself, others that it is an anonymous figure. What we can say for sure is that it is not – as is sometimes suggested – Charles Dickens. Apart from the fact that it looks nothing like Dickens, the great writer died long before Green wrote his book!

'Well stocked with all the latest fiction'

Above the picture is one of Bath's many ghost signs: you can just make out the words 'George Gregory, Book Store, Lending Library, Well stocked with all the latest fiction'.

Blind windows, the window tax and 'daylight robbery'

The Grove Street *trompe-l'œil* is painted onto a blind window. This is an architectural feature that has the design of a window but is not glazed and has no opening.

As you walk round Bath you'll notice that many Georgian houses have these windows, giving architectural uniformity to their facades but providing no light or ventilation to those within. There are two reasons for this seeming eccentricity, one aesthetic and the other legal.

In 1696 King William III introduced the window tax. There was no income tax at the time and the government wanted a source of income that reflected the prosperity of the householder. The tax was based on the number of windows in a house. When it was first introduced, the poorer houses paid 2 shillings a year; those with 10 to 20 windows paid an extra 4 shillings; and there was an additional 8-shilling charge for houses with more than 20 windows.

The new tax had the unintended consequence of prompting many householders to block up some of their windows. There was even a trend for new houses to be built with a certain number of blind windows that could later be opened up and glazed if the owner was feeling extravagant.

There were various changes to the legislation over the years. A new rule in 1747 stated that windows less than 12 inches apart could be counted as a single window. This encouraged thrifty homeowners to move their windows closer together: the government responded by imposing a width restriction on adjacent windows!

The window tax was very unpopular, possibly inspiring the term 'daylight robbery'. In 1797, William Pitt the Younger tripled the tax and it is said that a house in Beauford Square has a short poem scratched onto a back window: 'God gave us light and it was good. Pitt came and taxed it, damn his blood.' (Unfortunately this window is not visible to passers-by.)

The tax was finally repealed in 1851, partly due to pressure from those who argued that a lack of light led to ill health. However, you can still see its effect in many places. Beauford Square is a good example, with both blocked-up windows and windows placed close to one another.

In other cases, the blind windows were a deliberate design feature. Georgian architects were very keen to preserve symmetry and uniformity in their buildings and sometimes the facades of adjacent houses would be designed to give the appearance of a single building.

This occasionally meant that extra windows had to be added for balance. However, they would need to be blocked in if they were placed in front of areas not intended to be seen, such as party walls or chimney shafts. You can see an example of this at Claremont Place on Camden Road.

Over time, blind windows have come to be regarded as features in themselves. Some have been painted black to create the illusion of real windows when viewed from a distance. Other householders have gone further: one or two houses on London Road have added painted blinds and pull cords.

If you walk from London Road up Upper East Hayes, you'll spot another *trompe-l'œil*: a person standing by a window, but this time without a book.

'5792' INSCRIPTION

A house built in 5792?

22 Grove Street, BA2 6PJ

In a city where the builders were rightly proud of their work, you can expect to see numerous datestones inscribed with the year in which a building was constructed. Dates from the 18th or 19th century are commonplace, but prepare to do a double-take when you pass No. 22 Grove Street. Here the date above the door is 5792!

The building in question was constructed in the early 1980s but its history – and the curious dating – goes back much further. The original buildings on this site date from either 1788 or 1792 (more below) in an area known as Eveleigh's Wharf and were later known as Eveleigh's House and the Old Brewery.

The houses were on the edge of the Pulteney Estate, an ambitious attempt to create a Georgian new town in the village of Bathwick. Opposite Eveleigh's House was a new purpose-built prison, and the street was home to several inns – it is thought that No. 22 itself may at one time have been a coaching inn.

Whatever the original grand design, by the mid-20th century Grove Street was in decline and proposals were made for redevelopment. Eventually a compromise was reached whereby a new office block would be built, with a replica of the original facade and preserving some of the original stonework, including the datestone.

But why 5792? It is generally supposed that this is a reference to the chronology devised in the 17th century by Bishop James Ussher, Primate of All Ireland and a prolific scholar: after detailed research, he concluded that the Earth had been created in 4004 BCE and that all events should be measured from this time. By this reckoning, 22 Grove Street would have been built in 1788, the year in which the Pulteney lease was signed.

However, an alternative theory is that the date refers to the Masonic calendar. In some ways this is more likely, as many of Bath's 18th-century architects were (or at least are thought to have been) Freemasons.

Just to confuse matters further, different groups of Masons have different calendars, but it's likely that the Craft Masons' system is the one in use here. This would start counting at 4000 BCE, meaning that 22 Grove Street was built in 1792. There is no firm evidence either way, so you can take your pick.

SENSORY GARDEN

A garden for all the senses

Henrietta Park, Henrietta Street, BA2 6LS
henriettapark.org
8am until dusk

Henrietta Park is quiet and secluded, a place for dog walkers, nature lovers and anyone in search of a bit of peace and quiet. Hidden in one corner is an area specifically created for tranquillity, a fenced-off area designed to engage all the senses.

The park opened in 1897 to celebrate Queen Victoria's Diamond Jubilee. It was named after Henrietta Laura Pulteney, the daughter of Sir William Pulteney who built the nearby Bathwick Estate. Today it is full of mature trees, shrubberies and flowerbeds, with benches and lawns for picnicking.

The sensory garden (also known as the Garden of Remembrance) was created as a memorial to King George V in 1937. It was later redesigned as a garden for blind people, with an emphasis on sweetly-smelling plants.

Today the focus is on all the senses, making this a place for mindful reflection and relaxation. At the centre of the garden is a pond with lilies, a fountain and a sundial. Trellises and seats around the pond provide a shady place to sit.

Grass and flowerbeds surround the pond. And around the edge of the garden is a semi-wild area with trees, creating a tiny woodland space. It is all visually attractive. The blocks of vivid colour in the flowering plants may be designed for the partially sighted but will surely appeal to all.

But the other senses are catered for as well. Listen for the different sounds: the trickling of the fountain, birdsong, the distant barking of dogs and insects buzzing about. Then there are the scented plants and herbs, including lavender and mint. You'll even feel different textures beneath your feet, with grass, paving stones and gravel, and earth and twigs between the trees.

You may see people sitting on the benches and talking quietly or just taking time out to read a book. But everyone obeys the injunction at the entrance to keep noise to a minimum.

Although Henrietta Park is open 24/7, the sensory garden closes at dusk. To find the garden, enter the park by the entrance on Henrietta Street opposite Bathwick Villas.

WALCOT WALL

Who are those stone faces?

Walcot Street (opposite Julian House charity shop), BA1 5LZ

As you walk into Bath along Walcot Street, you'll notice that the right-hand side of the road is a massive retaining wall, built to support the multi-storey houses of The Paragon, towering high above. The wall is astonishing enough, but look closely as you approach the Ladymead Fountain and you'll spot a series of carved faces attached to the stone. Who are they and why are they there?

The first of these faces (or 'gargoyles' as they're sometimes incorrectly known) were carved 'for fun' by Paul Rogers, a local stonemason, in the 1980s. His collection of four figures was neglected and forgotten until another mason – Paul Bloomfield – added to them in 2013.

At that time, Walcot had started to rebrand itself as Bath's artisan quarter, as it's still known today. The stone faces project was the brainchild of Martin Tracy of The Framing Workshop at No. 80. He persuaded 20 of his fellow independent traders to model for a new series of faces, to showcase the range of businesses in the area and to attract visitors. The result was a mixture of caricatures and comic, mythological or symbolic representations, an invitation to guess who was who.

Look out for the Shady Lady in her oversized glasses, and Egg-Head, who represents the Natural Theatre Company (at that time located on Walcot). Then there is the Green Warrior, almost obscured by foliage, one of Rogers' originals …

Incidentally, the Wall of Walcot continues to be a place to discover local talent. In 2022 the Traders' Committee launched an exhibition called the Open Air Art Gallery, using the wall to display works by local artists. It is hoped this will be the first of many such events.

MUSEUM OF BATH ARCHITECTURE

Fascinating museum in a Gothic Revival chapel

The Countess of Huntingdon's Chapel, The Paragon, The Vineyards, BA1 5NA
01225 333895
museumofbatharchitecture.org.uk
admin@bptrust.org.uk
By appointment (charges apply)

The Museum of Bath Architecture is doubly interesting. First there is the museum collection, a treasure trove of material about the Georgian city. Then there is the history and the architecture of the building itself.

The museum is housed in the Countess of Huntingdon's Chapel, built for Selina Hastings in 1765. The countess appears to have been a formidable woman. She was extremely rich, well-connected and determined to improve the world. She was a follower of John Wesley and his Nonconformist Methodism and used her wealth to finance orphanages, overseas missions and the building of chapels.

The chapel in Bath, which adjoined Lady Huntingdon's own home, is the only one of her Methodist chapels that remains today. It was intended 'to protect the residents from the evils of Bath society', so it is slightly ironic that it should have become one of the most fashionable places of worship in the city.

The building has arched windows and an embattled facade and it features Gothic motifs rather than the Greek and Roman styles that were popular at the time. This makes it a rare example of 18th-century Gothic Revival architecture in Bath.

The chapel was last used for worship in 1981. It was subsequently acquired by the Bath Preservation Trust and opened as a museum in 1992. Although it was extensively restored, the interior was kept virtually intact, retaining the pulpit, lecterns and gallery and many original decorative features.

The Museum of Bath Architecture tells the story of Georgian architecture and covers the creation of the city, its built heritage and the impact of Georgian design on the present day. The museum's many exhibits include a scale model of Bath, giving a bird's-eye view of the entire city, models of Georgian houses, and information about Bath stone and 18th-century construction techniques.

Although the museum no longer has regular opening times, you can make an appointment to consult the extensive archives and to use the library. Tours of the museum can also be arranged, although charges apply (see website for details). And, of course, you can stand outside at any time and marvel at the Countess of Huntingdon's Chapel.

TURNING CIRCLE

An inverted bow window

114–116 Walcot Street, BA1 5BG
(now a lighting shop)

Walcot Street is notable both for its independent and artisan shops and for the individual architecture of its buildings. One building that might strike you as particularly quirky is the lighting shop at 114–116 Walcot Street (also known as Cornwell Buildings) with its rather unusual concave bow window, curving inwards rather than the more usual outwards.

Originally the Walcot Wine Vaults, the building dates from 1820. It operated as a wine merchant and then as a pub, finally closing in 1914. It was then converted into a shop.

But why the unusual shop front? In fact, this was not an architectural whim or even anything to do with the Walcot Wine Vaults. The answer is in the building across the road, the Bell Inn. The Bell was once a coaching inn, and horses were stabled in the Bell Yard, directly opposite the wine vaults. The road was not wide enough for the horses and coaches to turn around, so they were forced to mount the pavement and use the space in front of the wine shop.

The coming of the railway to Bath made the stagecoaches redundant, and the last coach from London to Bath ran in 1843. The turning circle was no longer needed but the inverted bow window remains to this day.

The Bell Inn

The Bell was an important coaching inn and meeting place in the 18th and 19th centuries but its origins may go back to the 1500s. And although the coaches have long since disappeared, it remains a focal point for the local community.

In 2013 the Bell Inn was purchased by a group of more than 500 supporters. It was the first cooperative pub in Bath and at the time this was the largest pub buyout in Britain. It is now known as a slightly quirky live music venue and real ale pub.

WILLIAM BURGES WINDOW

A rare piece of stained glass

Bath Aqua Studio
105–107 Walcot Street, BA1 5BW
bathaquaglass.com
Shop: Mon–Sat 9.30am–5pm, Sun 10am–5pm

Bath Aqua on Walcot Street is a glass-blowing studio that creates a range of jewellery, gifts and glass homeware. It is also home to a rare and exquisite piece of stained glass by the Victorian designer William Burges.

You can see the Burges window at any time during opening hours. Walk through the cafe at the front of Bath Aqua to the glass-blowing studio, and the window is on the wall on your right. You may also have the opportunity to watch the glass-blowers at work.

The window was discovered by accident in 2009 during renovation work in the vaults beneath the Bath Abbey Chambers. In fact it might still be there, unnoticed, if a glass expert from Bath Aqua had not been present when what appeared to be no more than a rather grubby window was first spotted.

The stained-glass window was removed and taken to the studio for specialist cleaning. It soon became obvious that Bath Aqua had a very fine piece of glass on their hands, but what exactly was it and what was its history?

By a stroke of good fortune, the Antiques Roadshow television programme arrived in Bath in 2010 and the glass window was physically taken to the Assembly Rooms for examination. Experts on the show confirmed that this was an original design by William Burges, an architect who designed everything from buildings to windows to furniture and jewellery.

It was established that this window was very similar to one in Cardiff Castle, known to be by Burges. However, although many of his artworks are still in existence, very few of his glass pieces seem to have survived, so this one was an exciting discovery.

Further research suggested that the window had been commissioned in the 1880s by Bath jewellers Mallet & Son for their shop in Milsom Street. It was created by a company called Saunders, who worked from Burges' design. But how it later got from Milsom Street to the Abbey Chambers is a bit of a mystery.

The window has four central panels with figures engaged in different artistic pursuits. Around the edge are brightly coloured images of sapphires, rubies and emeralds, ideal for a jewellers' shop.

THE STAR INN

A curious shape for a pub

23 Vineyards, BA1 5NA
Mon–Sat 12 noon–12 midnight, Sun 12 noon–10.30pm

The Star Inn on Vineyards is a proper old-fashioned pub, one of the oldest in Bath. It is full of curiosities, not least of which is its rather curious shape.

The Star was constructed around 1760 by Daniel Aust, the builder responsible for a group of houses across the road at The Paragon. His workmen had to come into the pub each week to pick up their wages; presumably Aust hoped they would spend some of their hard-earned money on his beer rather than in the other nearby hostelries.

It was (and still is) a narrow building divided into four separate bars. The interior was refitted in the 19th century by Gaskell and Chambers, who were responsible for many of the country's Victorian pubs. It has changed little since then. The oak panelling and the wooden benches are still there, and the rooms are numbered, as was once required by the licensing laws.

Sitting in The Star today, you can almost imagine yourself back in the days of Daniel Aust and his thirsty workers. It's not just the period fittings, but the lack of music, television or games machines. This is a place where people come for a drink and a chat or even a game of dominoes.

One bar is so small that it holds just a single bench, ominously nicknamed 'death row'. Another has press cuttings and architectural drawings on the walls so you can study the history of the pub at your leisure.

But what of The Star's peculiar shape? A long, thin structure that, seen from above, looks almost exactly like a coffin? Of course, it might simply be that the building had to be fitted into a rather confined space. Or – according to some – it was because Daniel Aust wanted to advertise the other side of his business. As well as a builder, he was also a coffin-maker!

MUSEUM OF BATH AT WORK

A real-tennis court that became a factory that became a museum

Julian Road, BA1 2RH
bath-at-work.org.uk
Daily 10.30am–5pm in summer; see website for winter opening times
Entrance charge
Bus 31 to Alfred Street, then 4-min. walk

Tucked away between Julian Road and Lansdown Road, the Museum of Bath at Work deserves to be much better known. It is one of those rare cases where the building itself is just as interesting as its contents. Not only does it showcase the industrial history of Bath, but it has been part of that history itself, charting the city's journey from leisure resort to industrialisation and back to leisure.

Built in 1777, this was the largest real-tennis court in the country, intended as part of a leisure complex alongside a riding school and a horse exercise yard. It proved financially unsuccessful and was subsequently put to other uses, including a circus, a school and various industrial functions such as a brewery and a soap factory.

By the 1970s the building was derelict, causing a headache for the city council, which realised that its structure and layout made it impractical for most modern purposes. But by a tremendous piece of serendipity, the charitable trust that became the Museum of Bath at Work was at the same time looking for a home.

The trust had acquired an extraordinary collection comprising the entire factory contents of J. B. Bowler's soft drinks works on Avon Street. They were now able to recreate the factory exactly as it had been when it closed in 1969, including numerous miscellaneous artefacts that might have been lost if Mr Bowler and his descendants had not been inveterate hoarders!

Better still, the new museum had space for exhibitions about the city's industrial history – did you know that both plasticine and the Pitman shorthand method were invented here? More recent temporary exhibitions have expanded the museum's coverage, including subjects such as housework and women's war activities.

The museum might be small, but it is crammed with all manner of objects designed to evoke the working city and working lives of the past.

LINK SNUFFERS

A relic of the days before street lighting

Outside several houses in the Upper Town
Look for examples in Alfred Street, River Street and Catherine Place

One of the many delights of Bath's Georgian architecture is the variety and craftsmanship of the ironwork outside the houses. There are railings, lamp overthrows and all manner of weird and wonderful door knockers. Occasionally you'll find an object whose purpose is more obscure – like the large conical link snuffers that can still be seen beside some of the doorways in the Upper Town.

These are a relic of the days before street lighting. If you didn't have your own carriage to take you home after an evening's entertainment at the theatre or the Assembly Rooms, you would have to walk or hire a sedan chair. Either way, you would require the services of a link boy to escort you through the dark streets.

The link boy would carry a lighted torch to guide the way and expose any would-be robbers that might be lurking in the shadows. Once you had been safely delivered to your home, the torch could be extinguished in the specially designed snuffer.

The link boy and the sedan bearers (if you had taken a chair) would then be left to find their own way back in the darkness. Presumably the cost of the extra wax was more important to them – or to their masters – than their own safety.

Although the link snuffers (or 'candle snuffer-outers') no longer have any use, they are still a feature of several houses in the streets around The Circus and the Royal Crescent.

For even more curiosities, have a look at the house at No. 14 Alfred Street, BA1 2QX. Here there is a whole collection of ironwork, including two link snuffers and a large wrought-iron winch. This was used to lower goods down to the tradesman's entrance – unusually the house was built with no outside steps leading to the basement.

UNUSUAL BI DISCS
AT THE MUSEUM
OF EAST ASIAN ART

Mysterious Neolithic artefacts

12 Bennett Street, BA1 2QJ
meaa.org.uk
See website for opening hours
Entrance charge
Bus 6A from Guildhall to Alfred Street

© MEAA

UNUSUAL BI DISCS
AT THE MUSEUM
OF EAST ASIAN ART

Mysterious Neolithic artefacts

12 Bennett Street, BA1 2QJ
meaa.org.uk
See website for opening hours
Entrance charge
Bus 6A from Guildhall to Alfred Street

© MEAA

The Museum of East Asian Art (MEAA) is full of traditional artefacts from the earliest times to the present day. But among the ceramics, bronzes and bamboo carvings are some more unusual items. The museum is home to four mysterious Chinese 'bi discs' from the Neolithic era.

Bi discs are flattened rings carved from jade or other hard stone. They were often found in tombs, placed around the feet or stomach of the dead person. Because jade is difficult to work, it is assumed that the discs were valuable and that they must have had some ritual significance. It is further speculated that the round shape signified the sky, but no one knows for sure.

What we do know is that there is a long tradition of burying objects with the dead, and that the use of bi discs is mentioned in the 2nd-century BCE textbook *The Rites of Zhou*, which describes them as a sacrifice to heaven. Perhaps they were intended to provide some kind of assistance in the afterlife?

Whatever their exact purpose, bi discs continued in use until the Han Dynasty (which ended in 220 CE). Those in the MEAA, however, have been dated to Neolithic times (approx. 6000–1700 BCE.) Two of them are fashioned from jade and two from green serpentine, a similarly hard material.

It was only in the 20th century that bi discs were first found in tombs, and it was some time before academics and collectors started to take an interest in them. So it is perhaps not surprising that they are a rarity in British museum collections. Bath residents are lucky that they caught the eye of the museum's founder.

The MEAA is based on the personal collection of Brian McElney, a prominent lawyer who worked in Hong Kong for many years and who remained actively involved with the museum until his death in 2023. Today it contains 2,000 items and is the only UK museum dedicated to the art and culture of East and South-East Asia.

Acorns, animals and Masonic symbols

The Circus, BA1 2ET

The Circus is one of the best-known addresses in Bath but few visitors stop to look at the intricate detail of the houses. The acorns on the parapets are obvious enough, but why are they there? Even more intriguing is the frieze that runs all the way around, above the Doric columns of the ground floor. Look closely and you'll see that it contains 525 separate images, all of them different from one another.

These images include animals, birds and serpents. There are flowers, vases and musical instruments. Then there are nautical and scientific instruments, and esoteric symbols. Many of these designs were copied

from George Wither's *A Collection of Emblemes*, published in 1635, but there is clearly also some iconography at work here. However, opinions vary as to exactly what this is.

First, there is the druidic influence. We know that John Wood the Elder, who designed The Circus, was fascinated by the druids and that he wrote a book suggesting that Bath had once been a druidic centre. The acorns are an obvious reference; less obvious to the uninitiated is the fact that the dimensions of The Circus are almost identical to those of Stonehenge (assumed by many to have been built by druids).

However, it is also thought that Freemasonry was a major factor in the design. We don't know for certain whether John Wood was a Freemason, but the inclusion of Masonic symbols in the frieze does seem to indicate this.

Look out in particular for the ouroboros (a snake circling the sun). The snake eating its own tail had been regarded as a symbol of infinity and rebirth since Egyptian times, but by the 18th century it had come to be adopted as a part of Masonic iconography.

There may be a further clue to Freemasonry in the layout of the Upper Town of Bath. Look at a map or an aerial photograph and you'll see that The Circus, Brock Street and the Royal Crescent join together to look exactly like a key. A second key is formed by The Circus, Gay Street and Queen Street. Keys are, of course, important Masonic symbols.

Yet another theory is that some of the images in the frieze are emblems of the medieval Knights Templar. We may never know exactly what mix of iconography influenced the choice of symbols or what they were intended to represent. But you can have fun walking around The Circus trying to identify the 525 different images.

For more information about the ourobouros, see the following double page.

The ouroboros: a symbol of divine enlightenment

In iconography and literature the circular figure of a serpent eating its own tail can sometimes be found.

The symbol is traditionally known as the 'ouroboros', a word taken from the Greek, but actually originating in Coptic and Hebrew, given that *ouro* means 'king' in Coptic and *ob* means 'snake' in Hebrew, combining to give us a 'royal serpent'. The reptile that raises its head above its body therefore serves as a symbol of mystic enlightenment. Within the framework of Hinduism it represents the sacred fire they call *kundalini*. Kundalini is how the Western medicine of the Middle Ages and Renaissance associated the bodily heat that rose from the coccyx to the cranium with the *venena bibas* (the imbibed venom spoken of by St Benedict of Nursia) of the snake whose bite is not cured with the same venom. In the same way that the Buddhist schools of spiritual enlightenment of the Dzogchen and Mahamudra reveal that the meditator should learn to 'bite his own tail like the serpent', the subject of the ouroboros and the imbibed venom remind us that spiritual enlightenment may only be attained by searching for a mental state beyond normal forms, where one looks inside oneself for true self-knowledge.

The Greeks popularised the term ouroboros in its literal sense, as 'he who eats his own tail'. They adopted this representation from the Phoenicians and Hebrews, who had in turn taken it from Egypt, where an ouroboros was depicted on a stele from as early as 1600 BCE. It represents Ra, the God of Light coming back to life from the shadows of night, which stand for death, thereby signifying the eternal return, life and death and a new start to existence. It also represents the reincarnation of the soul in successive physical bodies until it attains its optimal level of evolution, reaching bodily and spiritual perfection, an important subject for the peoples of the Orient and Middle East. As such, the snake eating its own tail may also be interpreted as an interruption in human development (represented by the serpent) to initiate the cycle of spiritual evolution (represented by the circle).

For Pythagoras it signified mathematical infinity, because the serpent as arranged in the form of a zero, an abstract number used to designate eternity, embodied in the ouroboros depicted as turning on itself.

The gnostic Christians identified it with the Holy Spirit, revealed by its wisdom as the Creator of all visible and invisible things, and whose greatest earthly expression is Christ. That's why in Greek gnostic literature this symbol is associated with the phrase '*Hen to pan*', meaning 'the all is one', and was adopted in the 4th and 5th centuries as an amulet that protected against evil spirits and venomous snakebites. This amulet was known as an Abraxas, the name of a god from the primitive gnostic pantheon which the Egyptians identified as Serapis, and it became one of the most famous talismans of the Middle Ages.

Greek alchemists were quick to adopt the figure of the ouroboros, and it even reached the hermetic philosophers of Alexandria, with whom Arab thinkers studied, introducing the image to their own schools of hermeticism and alchemy. These schools became famous, and Christians attended them in the Middle Ages. There is even historical evidence that members of the Order of the Templars, along with other Christian mystics, travelled to Cairo, Syria and even Jerusalem to be initiated in the hermetic sciences.

GEORGIAN GARDEN

A faithful re-creation of an 18th-century town garden

Behind No. 4 The Circus
Access from Gravel Walk in Victoria Park
bathnes.gov.uk/services/tourism-and-heritage/historic-parks-gardens/
georgian-garden
Daily 9am–5pm

Wherever you go in Bath, you're bombarded with information about the city's Georgian houses. However, less attention is paid to the gardens behind those houses, and the Georgian Garden is an attempt to correct that oversight.

Starting in the mid-1980s, the Georgian Garden was the first project of its kind in the UK. It is a re-creation of the garden that stood behind the house at No. 4 The Circus (now owned by Bath City Council). The project brought together archaeologists, archivists and garden historians, and between them they unearthed the original design of the garden.

Although changes had been made over the centuries, what you see today is as close as possible to the original layout, the space enjoyed by the first inhabitants when the house was built in 1760. More accurately, it copies the 1766 design, as at that time a set of steps was added to the back of the garden to allow access to Gravel Walk, a genteel walk into the city centre.

There are paths and box hedges, flowers and shrubs, all in a neat geometric design. Although it is impossible to know exactly what grew here in the 1760s, the 20th-century designers only used plants that were known to have been used at the time.

Surprisingly few people visit the Georgian Garden, so it is still a place to enjoy a bit of peace and quiet, to get a glimpse into the life of a society lady in 18th-century England. Perhaps, like Jane Austen's Emma, you will come away 'with spirits freshened, and thoughts a little relieved'.

The house itself at No. 4 The Circus is currently used by students at Bath Spa University. However it is occasionally opened during Heritage Weekends, giving visitors the opportunity to explore a typical Georgian house.

GREY PHONE BOX
ON BROCK STREET

An unusual colour for a phone box

Corner of Victoria Park on Brock Street, BA1 2LW

Telephone boxes were once a familiar feature of the urban environment, standing on every street corner, but they have mostly now disappeared. However, the phone box at the end of Brock Street, close to the Royal Crescent, is notable not for its survival but for its colour. It is not the classic Post Office red, but battleship grey.

You might think that phone boxes were always created to the same pattern. Not so: various shapes and designs (and even colours) were experimented with until the Post Office ran a competition for a new design in 1935. The winner was the architect Sir Giles Gilbert Scott, who came up with what was known as the K6, which became the prototype for all later installations.

Scott initially wanted his boxes to be painted grey but the Post Office had other ideas, insisting on red so that they would be clearly visible. Few houses at that time had their own telephones, so public phone kiosks were a lifeline for many. And, in an era before mobile phones, they were well used by people who were travelling or away from home.

Local folklore will tell you that the grey paint on the Brock Street box was the result of a bit of nimbyism on the part of Royal Crescent residents, who wanted a more subtle street view. This is not quite true, however, as the grey colour was actually adopted in beauty spots across the country. (There are a very few other survivors elsewhere in England.)

Today the Brock Street phone box continues to be painted grey with the bars around its windows picked out in red. It survived the Blitz and it even survived the indignity of being mistakenly repainted in Post Office red in 2003 (an error that was soon corrected).

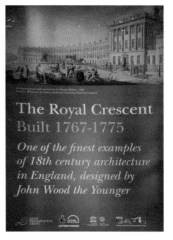

The Royal Crescent Built 1767-1775

One of the finest examples of 18th century architecture in England, designed by John Wood the Younger

Unlike other phone kiosks that have escaped demolition, this one has not been converted to an alternative use. Instead it celebrates the area's architectural heritage: look through the window and you'll see a poster with a drawing dated 1769 showing the construction of the Royal Crescent.

THE FRONT DOOR
OF NO. 22 ROYAL CRESCENT

The infamous yellow door

22 Royal Crescent, BA1 2LT

One of the defining characteristics of Georgian architecture is its uniformity. Bath, in particular, is renowned for the way that individual buildings are part of a visually harmonious landscape. So it is all the more surprising that one of the city's most famous sights – the Royal Crescent – should boast one front door that is a different colour from the rest.

Since John Wood the Younger created the Royal Crescent at the end of the 18th century, the convention has been to paint the doors in shades of white. But in 1972 Amabel Wellesley-Colley, the owner of No. 22, decided to have a yellow door. This, she said, had been the favourite colour of her famous ancestor, the Duke of Wellington.

There was an immediate outcry from outraged residents and from the Bath Preservation Trust. The city council responded by issuing an enforcement order requiring her to repaint the door in a more acceptable white. But Wellesley-Colley – by all accounts, a somewhat eccentric and formidable figure – stood firm.

She argued that it was her house and she had the right to paint the door – and even the windows if she wished – in any colour of her choice. Her appeal to the Secretary of State for the Environment became a bit of a *cause célèbre*, especially when she attended the resulting inquiry wearing a bright yellow suit. Rather surprisingly, Wellesley-Colley won her case and the door stayed yellow.

Although Amabel Wellesley-Colley moved out of the Royal Crescent many years ago, subsequent owners have retained the yellow door, although it now seems to be a more subtle shade than the original bright primrose. After all this time, perhaps it would cause an outcry if the famous coloured door returned to its original white!

THE URBAN GARDEN

A garden centre with a difference

Marlborough Buildings, BA1 2LZ
theurbangarden.org.uk
Thurs–Sat 10.30am–5pm, Sun 11.00am–4.30pm

Like any garden centre, the Urban Garden sells plants and seeds, ornaments and gifts. But that is where the similarity ends. This is a social enterprise, a not-for-profit set up for the benefit of the local community.

Situated at the heart of Victoria Park, the Urban Garden was established in 2021, its mission statement being: 'We take the power of plants and use it to help people grow.' It is staffed by volunteers and by people on work placements, who are given the skills they need to enhance their employment prospects. All the income is used to fund the garden's training schemes: City & Guilds programmes for people with mental health issues or other life challenges, and for the long-term unemployed.

Customers are welcome to browse and enjoy a drink in the cafe or chat to one of the garden experts who are on hand to answer questions. The Urban Garden is particularly popular with dog walkers, who pop in on their way through the park. A 'howl of fame' near the entrance has photographs of some of the regular canine visitors …

Because this is the centre of Bath, where many people live in flats, the Urban Garden sells lots of houseplants and plants designed for small spaces. And it encourages people to 'green up' in other ways: there are workshops on a range of subjects, from botanical drawing to making Christmas wreaths to 'how not to kill your houseplant'.

Sustainability is important here. Everything is grown without chemicals and the compost is peat-free. Customers can take their plants away in cardboard 'POSIpots' rather than the conventional plastic pots and compost is sold in refillable containers.

As no visit to a garden centre is complete without a purchase of soap, candles or household ornaments, you'll find a range of goods to choose from in the greenhouses. But in keeping with the Urban Garden's ethos as a community enterprise, they are all made by local artists and craftspeople. And they are chosen for being slightly quirky …

North

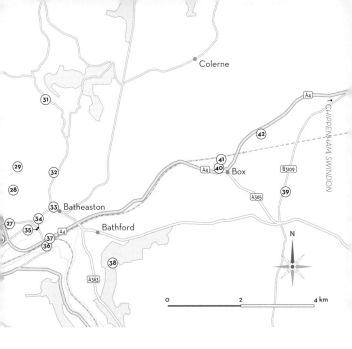

RED OCHRE TRAIL

The remains of ochre mining

Golden Valley Nature Reserve, High Street, Wick, BS30 5QJ
goldenvalley.org.uk/index.htm
Bus 620 from Guildhall to The Carpenters Arms
No car parking on site, but parking available beside Village Hall

Stone and mineral extraction tends to be associated with the southern side of Bath. But travel to the north and you'll find another natural resource: red ochre. If you visit the Golden Valley Nature Reserve, you can follow a Red Ochre Trail to explore the landscape where mining took place for almost 200 years.

Golden Valley is primarily a nature reserve built upon a formerly industrial area. Limestone, iron and ochre were once extracted in the valley, and in the 18th century a paper mill and ironworks were sited here. Today there are walks along the river and through woodland. Waymarked walks allow you to explore the area's industrial history: Ravens Rock takes you to the limestone quarry and the Red Ochre Trail follows the old ochre works.

Red ochre, used primarily as a pigment in the manufacture of paints, is known to have been mined at Golden Valley since at least 1800. The Golden Valley Ochre & Oxide Co Ltd was established in 1892 and continued to extract ochre from surface pits and underground mines until the 1970s.

The Red Ochre Trail is an easy (and fully accessible) route through the abandoned works. It is immediately apparent that you are in an area rich with ochre because the ground is red underfoot. As you follow the route around, you'll see various industrial relics, including fragments of rail tracks and a turntable.

Halfway round you come to the weir. This was constructed in the 18th century to drive the mill but adapted in 1892 to provide additional power for the ochre works.

The Red Ochre Trail doubles up as a nature walk (it is also known as the 'bat trail'). You'll see a wide variety of trees, grasses and wild flowers and you may also spot some of the many species of birds, insects and other wildlife that frequent the area.

For those who can cope with steep slopes and rough paths, Golden Valley offers many miles of trails through varied scenery with rocks, cliffs and a reservoir. The high point (literally) is the Ravens Rock viewpoint.

SIR BEVIL GRENVILLE'S MONUMENT

The oldest war memorial in Britain

On the Cotswold Way, near Lansdown Road, BA1 9DD
Bus 620 from Guildhall to Battlefields; nearest car park Lansdown Road,
2.7 km away

It might seem that the only people who ever pass Sir Bevil Grenville's monument, on a footpath on Lansdown Hill, are walkers on the long-distance Cotswold Way from Bath to Chipping Campden. Yet this ornate monument with its adulatory inscription is the oldest existing war memorial in Britain. It is also – some might say – testament to an act of heroic recklessness.

The monument stands in the Battlefields area to the north of Bath, where the Civil War Battle of Lansdown was fought in 1643.

Sir Bevil Grenville was a landowner and member of parliament who led a band of Cornish pikemen as part of a Royalist advance on the city of Bath. As they approached the city, the Parliamentary army had already adopted a strategic position on the top of Lansdown Hill. Undeterred, Sir Bevil led his men up the hill, but they were soon beaten back. They tried again, with an equal lack of success. It was at the third attempt that he – and many of his troops – died in hand-to-hand combat.

Technically the Battle of Lansdown is regarded as a Royalist victory, as the Parliamentarians subsequently retreated. However, the victory came at the cost of great loss of life, and of course the Royalist army later lost the war.

Sir Bevil himself might have been relegated to a footnote in history if it hadn't been for his grandson, George Granville, who erected a flamboyant monument to his memory in 1720. The 7.6-metre-high Baroque structure is decorated with a griffin and various coats of arms. The inscriptions include a rather effusive description of the battle, Sir Bevil's part in it, and his life and character more generally. They also – incidentally or otherwise – make mention of George Granville's own status and achievements.

Sir Bevil Grenville's monument is a few minutes' walk from Lansdown Road. You could either get there by bus or car or take the meandering 12-km walk along the Cotswold Way from Bath Abbey. Coming this way, you'll pass several markers and information boards showing key points in the Battle of Lansdown. You'll also have the benefit of some spectacular views.

KELSTON LOCK-UP

A place to sleep off the drink

Bath Road, Kelston, BA1 9AQ
Bus 19 from Westgate Buildings to the Old Crown

On the main road through Kelston, not far from the Old Crown Inn, is a small windowless building. A sign on the door tells you that this was the village lock-up, a place where miscreants could be held overnight.

Lock-ups were once a common sight in small villages where there was no police station and it was too far to walk to the nearest prison or magistrate's court. People who were drunk or unruly would be held in the lock-up until they had sobered up. It was also a convenient place to keep offenders who were due to be committed for trial.

The Kelston lock-up was probably built in the late 18th century. This was a time when rural crime was rising, partly due to an increase in itinerant labour. Drunkenness was also a problem throughout the country; the proximity of the lock-up to the village pub may not have been a coincidence.

From the outside, it is an unprepossessing building, built from thick rubble with a gabled roof. The wooden door has an iron grille and strong locks and hinges. This isn't a place that you could escape from easily. If the door is open, you may be able to peek inside. You'll see that there are two separate vaulted cells so that more than one prisoner could be detained if necessary. You'll also note that it is dark, damp and ill-ventilated – not somewhere you would choose to spend the night!

The village pound

A small patch of grass at the side of the lock-up would once have been the village pound. Probably dating from medieval times, this is where stray cattle and other animals were kept until claimed by their owners. It would have been surrounded by high walls to prevent the animals from escaping but – unlike their human neighbours – they would at least have had the benefit of plentiful light and ventilation.

SALTFORD BRASS MILL

An early manufacturing process

The Shallows, Saltford, BS31 3EX
brassmill.com
May–Oct: see website for dates
Bus A4 from Terrace Walk to The Shallows

At the beginning of the 18th century, several water mills along the River Avon between Bath and Bristol were converted for use in the brass industry. Only one of those mills remains – the Saltford Brass Mill – and it is now open as a museum showcasing an early manufacturing process.

There had been a mill at Saltford since medieval times. The earliest mention is in the Domesday Book. It was originally a grist mill and then a fulling mill (for cleaning and processing wool) before it was leased by the Bristol Brass Company in 1721.

The Bristol Brass Company was engaged in the now-notorious 'triangular' trade between Bristol, Africa and the West Indies. The mills along the Avon would produce brass artefacts that were highly prized in Africa. These were traded for enslaved persons who were taken to the Caribbean and exchanged for goods such as sugar or tobacco.

The manufacture of brass pans, bowls and other items was part of an early industrial process that anticipated the Industrial Revolution. After the abolition of slavery, however, the Bristol Brass Company failed to take advantage of new opportunities. Its mills were sold and their activities gradually ceased.

The Saltford mill managed to escape demolition because in 1928 it was purchased by Eric Butler, a local businessman with an interest in sport. He converted it into a squash court and bowling alley, using the waterwheel to generate electricity for the lighting.

The mill is now leased by the local authority and run as a museum by a team of volunteers. On Open Days visitors can see the waterwheel in action. The leats (artificial watercourses conducting water to the mill) and the sluice gates are visible, as is the massive annealing furnace in which metal was heated to make it easier to work.

Information boards tell the story of the mill and the brass industry. You'll learn how the mill rolled brass into sheets and manufactured artefacts for export. Tools used in the manufacturing process, and some of the items created, are on display. And you can even see the outline of the squash court that saved Saltford Brass Mill from destruction.

FAIRFIELD HOUSE

Former home of Emperor Haile Selassie

2 Kelston Road, BA1 3QJ
fairfieldhousebath.co.uk
Guided tours of the house most Sundays
Bus 21 from Westgate Buildings to Rudmore Park, then 13-min. walk

Bath has had its fair share of royal visitors over the centuries, but one of the most surprising must be the Ethiopian Emperor Haile Selassie, who lived at Fairfield House between 1936 and 1941. You might wonder why a foreign ruler would choose to spend several years living in a Victorian villa in a quiet suburb of Bath. The answer is that he and his family were forced into exile following Italy's invasion of Ethiopia.

Fairfield House was an ideal choice. It was secluded, on the edge of the city, with wonderful views that are said to have reminded the emperor of Ethiopia. And it was close enough to Bath for him to be treated at the Mineral Hospital for the mustard burns he had suffered before leaving his country.

When Haile Selassie returned on a state visit to the UK in 1954, he visited Bath and was given the Freedom of the City. Such was his affection for the place that when he died, he left Fairfield House to the city of Bath 'for the good of the elderly'. That is still the primary use of the house, which has been providing a day service for the last 30 years. It is also a multicultural meeting place, catering for locals, Rastafari and the Ethiopian community in Bath.

Tours of the house – and Caribbean lunches

Fairfield House is open most Sundays for tours exploring the legacy of Haile Selassie. Visitors can walk around the house and grounds and enjoy the exhibitions. A Caribbean lunch is available in the cafe. The tours are an 'immersive experience' (with costumes and music) to allow visitors to discover what life was like for the Ethiopian royal family in Britain. You'll see the accommodation lived in by the emperor and his family, including a shrine in the Empress Menen's room. A small museum area has information, artefacts and a large portrait of the emperor himself.

Behind the house are the sacred garden and the Haile Selassie Peace Garden, built in 2014 and featuring a number of exotic plants. And you can still admire the views that once reminded an emperor of home.

ART AT THE HEART

A fascinating hospital art collection

Royal United Hospital, Combe Park, BA1 3NG
artatruh.org
Corridor leading off from the main entrance, at any reasonable time
Bus 4a from Westgate Buildings, or drive and park in pay-and-display car park

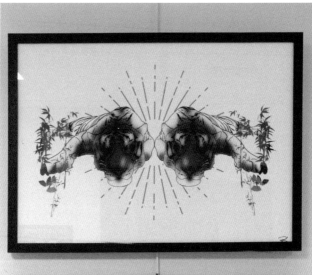

Pictures by Tracy Recce-Oliviere – Bath Mind exhibition in 2023: 'Art as Therapy'

A hospital may not be the obvious place for a contemporary art gallery. But for the last 20 years, the Royal United Hospital in Bath has been home to a huge variety of artworks, some specially commissioned and some on sale to the public.

This is the work of Art at the Heart, an ambitious programme that displays art throughout the hospital as well as providing music and art on the wards, with art therapy and occasional performances. The aim is to use art to create an educational and therapeutic environment, to enhance the patient and staff experience.

As you walk through the hospital, you'll see art everywhere. The corridors are lined with paintings and photographs. There are display cases with ceramics and other artefacts. And wherever there's an open space, there's likely to be a sculpture. You will also spot colourful displays of children's artwork from local schools.

As well as enhancing the environment, the art collection has the benefit of raising much-needed money for the hospital (which receives a commission on sales). Art at the Heart also supports local artists and works closely with the charity Mind to promote mental well-being within the community.

Although the RUH's artworks are primarily aimed at patients, visitors and staff at the hospital, the general public can walk along the central corridor behind the Atrium cafe to enjoy the items on show. This is the main display area, with exhibitions changing every three months. Sometimes these are touring exhibitions but they are more likely to be work by local artists.

Many of the pictures and other artworks are for sale. Who knows, perhaps you'll go away with an addition to your living-room walls!

TOMB OF BLATTENGETA HEROUY WOLDE SELASSIE

The Ethiopian Foreign Minister who died in Bath in 1938

Locksbrook Cemetery, Upper Bristol Road, BA1 3DQ
Apr–Sept 8.30am–7.30pm, Oct–Mar 8.30am–4pm
Bus X39 from Westgate Buildings

Among the ornamental Victorian tombs, simple headstones and towering trees of Locksbrook Cemetery, one grave immediately catches the eye. This was the original burial place of Blattengeta Herouy Wolde Selassie, the Ethiopian Foreign Minister who died in Bath in 1938.

Blattengeta Herouy was an eminent scholar and historian (his title Blattengeta means 'chief of the wise men'). He was also a diplomat and a politician and a close personal friend of Emperor Haile Selassie. He joined the emperor during his exile at Fairfield House in Bath (see p. 152) and remained there until his death at the age of 60.

Blattengeta Herouy was buried at Locksbrook Cemetery in what was clearly a grand ceremony. The emperor himself addressed the mourners, surrounded by priests in black robes with colourful stoles. Lit tapers were held by the people standing around the coffin. It was reported that the emperor's voice broke as he delivered the oration and that the empress was in tears throughout.

This was not to be Blattengeta Herouy's final resting place, however. In the 1950s his body was exhumed and flown to Addis Ababa for reburial in the land of his birth. But the grave in Locksbrook Cemetery remained and was fully restored in 2016.

Red, green and gold: the official colours of the Rastafari religion

The gravestone has inscriptions in both Amharic (the official language of Ethiopia) and English. It is swathed in bands of red, green and gold, the official colours of the Rastafari religion.

Locksbrook Cemetery is now closed to new graves and has been designated a 'Nature Conservation Site'. Visitors can walk between the graves and marvel at the ornate decorated tombs (carved angels seem to be particularly popular here). A particular feature of the cemetery are the trees, some of which are very old, with several planted in memory of the dead. There are several unusual species to be spotted: look out for several giant sequoias, Japanese cherry and red cedars.

FORMER HERMAN MILLER FACTORY

Imaginative repurposing of a modern factory building

Bath Spa University, Locksbrook Campus, Locksbrook Road, BA1 3EL
Cafe and bookshop open to the public on weekdays
Bus 5 from James Street West to Burnham Road

The Herman Miller factory on Locksbrook Road was an innovative piece of industrial design. It has now been repurposed as the Locksbrook Campus of Bath Spa University, a stunning adaptation that has won many awards.

The factory was built in 1975 for Herman Miller, a manufacturer of office furniture, and was at the forefront of contemporary industrial architecture. Like the nearby Bath Cabinet Makers factory, it was intended to create a pleasant working environment. However, it was also designed with flexibility in mind; the structure incorporated movable panels and doors, making it easy to adapt the internal layout as circumstances changed.

When the factory building was acquired by Bath Spa University in 2016 to accommodate the Schools of Art and Design, some changes were necessary. In particular, the university needed a greater floor area and much more natural light. Because the factory had been designed for flexibility, it was possible to do this while retaining the original design.

Today the Locksbrook Campus is an eye-catching building, an imaginative use of space that makes it ideal for design students. It includes open-plan workspaces and social areas that can be seen from all floors and are able to accommodate a wide variety of activities.

The building is still to some extent a work in progress but you can see how it has been adapted to be ideally suited to creative work. Students can work independently or collaboratively and the ability to see what others are doing allows for more spontaneous interactions.

A particular feature of the repurposed building is the original concrete factory floor, showing that even as a modern structure it retains some of its history. It is not surprising that the Locksbrook Campus should have won several architectural awards, recognising factors such as innovation and sustainability.

Members of the public are welcome to visit the cafe and the bookshop on weekdays. From here you can see the whole building and get a sense of the creative activity all around you. At certain times of year, you may also be able to view exhibitions of the students' work.

COLOSSAL HEAD OF JUPITER

A statue hidden among the trees

The Great Dell, Victoria Park, BA1 2LZ
Bus 6 from Bath Abbey to Belvedere, then 15-min. walk

First opened in 1830, Victoria Park was the earliest municipal park in England. Today it is the largest and most popular park in Bath. But that doesn't stop it being full of surprises and hidden spaces. One of the less frequented corners is the Great Dell, and nestling between the tall trees of the Dell is the Colossal Head of Jupiter.

The Great Dell is the enclosed sunken space between the Botanical Gardens and Weston Road. A former stone quarry, it was landscaped by William Beckford (see p. 164) in the mid-19th century and planted with a mixture of trees, including some North American conifers and rare specimens. The area was later incorporated into the Botanical Gardens.

The Dell is a quiet and secluded area, with an elevated walkway that allows you to look down on the trees. The first thing you see when you walk through the gate is a stone memorial to William Shakespeare, erected in 1864, 300 years after the playwright's birth. However, a much larger and more impressive monument, the Colossal Head of Jupiter, is hidden among the trees to the right.

This statue is indeed colossal. Fashioned out of Bath stone, it stands 6 metres above the ground and weighs a massive 5.44 tonnes. It was the work of a local sculptor, John Osborn, who died in 1838 leaving his widow and family penniless. A public subscription was immediately launched to purchase the statue and provide for the family. The sum of £100 (worth around £13,000 today) was raised and Jupiter was moved to the Dell in 1839.

Colossal or otherwise, Jupiter isn't as visible as he might be. You may catch glimpses of him from the road or from outside the fence as you approach the Great Dell. But if you stand directly in front of the statue, his face is partly obscured by leaves and branches so that he seems more like the Green Man than a Roman god. To see him in his full glory, you need to walk around the back and view him in profile!

MINERVA SCULPTURE

A wooden owl with a great view

Primrose Hill Community Woodland, Fonthill Road, BA1 5RH
primrosehillwoodland.com
Bus 31 (park-and-ride) from Milsom Street to Kingswood School

Primrose Hill Community Woodland has everything you could wish for: a hidden location, a wide variety of native trees and plants, and wonderful views. And a wooden owl named Minerva.

The woodland was created as a community project to mark the millennium in 2000. Nearly 8 hectares of meadowland were leased from a local landowner, and the planting began. Today the site has more than 20,000 trees, mostly native species, and a wide variety of shrubs.

As you approach – along a quiet road past Kingswood School and Chelscombe Farm – you become aware that this is a peaceful haven. Come on a weekday afternoon in the spring and you may have the place to yourself, with no sound but the birds chattering in the trees.

You can stroll between the trees or just sit quietly on a bench near the pond. Or you could climb an uphill path all the way to Beckford's Tower (see p. 164). But whichever way you go, you are likely to be surprised by the large wooden sculpture of an owl. This was carved by local sculptor Nic Cozins to mark the 20th anniversary of the Primrose Hill Woodland. It stands almost 2 metres high and was fashioned from the stump of a 90-year-old tree that had been a casualty of ash dieback.

The public were invited to suggest names for the owl and the most popular was Minerva (an appropriate Bath name – see below). But you might be tempted to think that she is not as wise as her name suggests, as she has her back firmly turned away from the glorious view of Kelston Round Hill in the distance behind her.

Minerva and Bath

Owls are traditionally associated with Minerva, the Roman goddess of wisdom. Minerva is also the goddess to whom the Roman Baths Temple was dedicated. You may sometimes also see a reference to Sulis Minerva. The Roman custom was to adopt local deities where possible, and here they combined Minerva with the Celtic goddess Sulis. Look out for a stone carving of Sulis Minerva in the Roman Baths Museum.

WILLIAM BECKFORD'S TOMB

Last resting place of a flamboyant eccentric

Lansdown Cemetery, BA1 9BH
Daily until dusk
Bus 31 (park-and-ride) from Milsom Street to Lansdown Cemetery

Beckford's Tower is a well-known feature of the Bath skyline, clearly visible at the top of Lansdown Hill. Less well known is the adjacent Lansdown Cemetery, once part of a pleasure garden and the final resting place of William Beckford.

Even by Bath standards, Beckford was famously eccentric. Born in 1760, he was fabulously wealthy, having inherited a fortune derived from his family's sugar plantations in Jamaica. This allowed him to indulge his many interests, including writing (his most famous work was the Gothic novel *Vathek*), collecting and architecture. Unfortunately, he was notorious in his private life and was eventually ostracised due to numerous relationships with both men and women, including – allegedly – one with a 10-year-old boy.

Beckford lived his final years in Bath and constructed the folly now known as Beckford's Tower as a home for his art collection. During this time he also designed his own tomb – a large pink granite sarcophagus with bronze plates on either end. Each plate bears a coat of arms, with one carrying a quote from *Vathek*: 'Enjoying humbly the most precious gift of heaven to man – Hope'. As a commoner – and a disgraced one at that – Beckford was not technically entitled to arms, but that did not deter him!

During Beckford's lifetime, the sarcophagus was placed in the pleasure ground next to the tower. However, after his death it had to be moved to the Bath Abbey Cemetery as the land was not consecrated. It only returned when Beckford's daughter offered the pleasure ground as a new cemetery for the parish of Walcot on the understanding that her father's tomb would be restored to its original position.

Today the graveyard is one of the few remnants of Beckford's Ride, a long strip of gardens, orchards and fields that connected the tower to his home on Lansdown Crescent. Quite apart from Beckford's tomb – slightly set apart on a mound surrounded by a ditch – the cemetery is full of elaborate Victorian graves, with lots of pink granite in evidence.

Lansdown Cemetery also bills itself as a natural area, with numerous wild flowers and butterflies. And – a factor that must surely have influenced Beckford's choice of the site – anyone who visits will have spectacular views of the surrounding countryside.

THE HOLY WELL
OF CHARLCOMBE

An ancient well with healing properties for the eyes

In the grounds of St Mary's Church, Charlcombe Lane
Bus 6 to Solsbury Way, then 12-min. walk

Bath is known for its many wells and springs. One of the oldest is the Holy Well, in the grounds of the hidden church of St Mary in Charlcombe. It is also one of the most sacred, its water reputed to have healing properties.

St Mary's is the oldest church in Bath, predating even the abbey. The current building has Norman origins, but there is evidence of a religious community on this site as far back as the 7th century. Since early times, people would take water from the well as it was reputed to be good for the eyes. As late as the 20th century, people were still bringing bottles to use the water for the same purpose or as holy water in baptisms.

The well was originally in the grounds of the rectory but its future was threatened when the building was put up for sale in the 1980s. Protesters included a 'hermit' – a local artist who took up residence beneath a tree in the garden.

In 1986 the church obtained a court order to evict the hermit but the protests continued. Eventually a compromise was reached and the water was redirected to the well's current location at the bottom of a slope beneath the church.

The well was rededicated in 1989. The water now flows into two pools and the well is topped by a modern stone carving of the baptism of Christ. It is situated in a designated Quiet Garden, a place for private rest, prayer or reflection.

The Holy Well is still used for baptisms and for religious festivals including Ascension Day and Easter Sunday.

NEARBY

The modern pews inside St Mary's Church were made by Robert 'Mousey' Thompson, a Yorkshire furniture maker known for his oak church fittings and his trademark mouse motif. Look for the little carved mice beneath the seats.

ANNUAL TOAD MIGRATION IN CHARLCOMBE

An unusual road closure

*Charlcombe Lane, north of the junction with Richmond Road, BA1 5TT,
extending for around 800 metres
Around six weeks during February and March each year*

For a few weeks every year, an unusual road sign appears in the village of Charlcombe. The red triangle with a picture of an animal is a familiar warning to drivers to be on the lookout for wildlife and other non-human road users. In this case, however, the animal is not a deer or a horse but a toad.

One of the UK's most important toad migration routes passes through the village, forcing the animals to cross Charlcombe Lane on their way downhill to the lake where they breed. Although most of the migrators are toads, frogs and newts follow the same route.

The animals move slowly and often walk along the road for some distance. In the past, this unfortunately led to many of them being hit by cars. So the road is now closed to through traffic for around six weeks every year during February and March. And the warning signs remind local drivers to go slowly and carefully.

Part of the Toads on Roads project that protects toads and other amphibians around the UK, these road closures have been in operation for the last 20 years.

You will see the red triangles with a picture of a toad during the road closure period. However, as toads are nocturnal, your best chance of spotting them is at dawn or dusk. Volunteers come round each night with torches and buckets to collect the toads and take them down to the water.

In Praise of the MERCIES of GOD to MARY BOTHAMLEY the Devoted WIFE of the First Vicar of this Parish and for more than 15 years a diligent Worker in it Who in full Faith entered into the Everlasting Light at Midday Dec.ʳ 17.ᵗʰ 1895 Aged 54: This Memorial is here placed by her Husband.

THE OPUS SECTILE PANELS OF ST STEPHEN'S CHURCH

A treasure house of Gothic Revival design

Lansdown Road, BA1 5SX
01225 420946 – ststephensbath.org.uk
Open to visitors Sat and Sun; phone for access at other times
Bus 31 from Milsom Street; car parking outside church or in nearby streets

Walking around the centre of Bath, you are likely to spot the hillside church of St Stephen's in the distance. However, the exterior gives no clue as to what lies within, a real treasure house of Gothic Revival design.

Built in the 1840s, St Stephen's is best known for its remarkable stained glass: 25 windows handcrafted by some of the major Victorian workshops. But your attention might also be caught by the unusual opus sectile panels, pictures that appear at first glance to be a sort of mosaic but which are actually something quite different. Whereas mosaics are created from random fragments of stone, opus sectile (or 'cut work') uses larger pieces, individually shaped to fit the design. It is a laborious process: each piece is hand carved to the exact shape required.

In Roman times, opus sectile was used to create elaborate floors and pavements out of materials such as marble, shell and mother-of-pearl. Similar designs can be seen in later Byzantine and Italian churches, but the technique eventually fell out of fashion. It was revived in the 19th century by English artists of the Arts and Crafts movement.

The workshop of James Powell and Sons created their own style of opus sectile, which involved cutting, painting and firing individual ceramic pieces. This enabled them to produce ornate panels for several English churches, including St Stephen's. (Powell and Sons were also responsible for many of the St Stephen's windows.)

Look out particularly for the reredos and for the floral designs on either side of the altar. The picture on the opposite page, with its very Victorian angels, is at the centre of the west wall and was created in memory of Mary Bothamley, the wife of Hilton Bothamley, who became the first vicar of St Stephen's in 1880.

> If you visit the church when it's not busy, you may be able to persuade one of the friendly church wardens to let you into the upper gallery for a bird's-eye view of the St Stephen's art treasures. You'll also get to see a large Pre-Raphaelite-style painting with a hidden door leading to the bell tower.

THE HANGING BOGS OF BATH ⑮

Added extras for Georgian houses

Cavendish Road, BA1 2UB
Visible from the Victoria Park side of the road

Walk along the back of Cavendish Road, past the edge of Victoria Park, and you'll see what looks like a series of large boxes attached to the sides of the houses, halfway up and apparently unsupported. These are the inelegantly nicknamed 'hanging bogs of Bath'.

These structures are the result of an uneasy meeting between Georgian architecture and Victorian sanitation. It may be hard to imagine today, but even the grandest of Bath's Georgian houses were built without toilets or even an indoor water supply.

Most people would relieve themselves in an outdoor privy or outhouse. However, those who had servants to deal with the slops would use a chamber pot – in the bedroom at night or behind a screen in the dining room during the day. (The dining-room pot would even be used during meals – try not to think about that next time you read about a dinner party in a Jane Austen novel …)

By the mid-19th century, the build-up of waste in outdoor cesspits had given rise to health concerns. At the same time, plumbing had advanced to a point where indoor running water was a possibility and, for those who could afford it, an indoor toilet became the latest status symbol.

Where space was at a premium, it was logical to extend at the back of the house for the new bathrooms. But the solution adopted on Cavendish Road was unusual: build an extension halfway up the house without carrying it down to ground level.

Having the toilets higher up would have had the advantage of being close to the bedrooms for night-time visits. But you do wonder how secure it felt to sit on a new-fangled plumbed-in toilet for the first time, knowing that there was no visible support beneath you!

Today some of the hanging bogs have been boxed in, but others still cling precariously to the sides of houses, a reminder of different times and different customs.

SEDAN-CHAIR RAMP

How sedan chairs would avoid the steps in Georgian times

Portland Place, BA1 2RU
Bus 31 from Milsom Street to Lansdown Grove

Built by John Eveleigh in 1786, Portland Place is a smart terrace of 10 Georgian houses on the lower slopes of Lansdown Hill. Like many 18th-century developments, it was built on a raised pavement. Unlike others, the pavement was so high that a ramp was needed for people who could not manage the steps.

Raised pavements were a feature of Georgian architecture. When a new development was being planned the pavement would be built up, leaving the basements and gardens of the new houses at the original ground level. In some cases the road would also be elevated; in others, such as at Portland Place, the pavement was high above the road.

This was done partly for sanitary reasons, to keep damp and sewage away from the living area of the houses. It also gave the houses a grander appearance and provided their owners with a pleasant space to walk to and from their homes.

In Bath the damp and possibility of flooding were major considerations. This was even the case on the hillsides, where water could seep out between the bands of limestone and clay. And in a city with steep hills and an undulating landscape, raised pavements were also a way of creating a level surface on which to build.

At Portland Place the combination of a steep incline and uneven ground meant that the pavement was unusually high. Steps were built to provide access to the houses but many people found these difficult to negotiate. So a subscription was raised for the building of a ramp.

This was not an early instance of accessibility awareness, but more a need for the citizens of Portland Place to travel in comfort. The fashionable way to get around the city was by sedan chair (see p. 86) but even the most seasoned chair carrier must have struggled to get up the steps. It can hardly have been comfortable for those inside the chair either.

As befitted the houses of Portland Place, the double ramp at the centre of the terrace was itself imposing. It had a tall stone obelisk at either side, at one time topped by lamps. Although the sedan chairs have long fallen out of use, the ramp remains. It has now been fully restored and still makes it easier for the residents to reach their homes.

BATTLEMENTED LOOKOUT TOWER IN HEDGEMEAD PARK

Part of an elaborate retaining wall designed to stop the hill from sliding down to the road

Lansdown Road, BA1 5NG

At first glance, the battlemented lookout tower in Hedgemead Park looks like the remains of some ancient fortifications. Or the sight of children pretending to fire arrows through a narrow loophole might suggest that it is an elaborately constructed play area. However, the truth is rather more prosaic: it is part of a retaining wall designed to stop the hill from sliding down to the road.

It is hard to imagine now, but in the 1870s almost 300 new homes were built on the slope that now comprises Hedgemead Park. These were small dwellings designed to accommodate the city's growing working class. Unfortunately, the land was unstable and several minor landslips threatened the safety of the houses and of the people who lived in them.

A major landslide following a gas leak in 1883 finally persuaded the local authority to evacuate the area. Miraculously, most of the damage was to the houses rather than the residents, but many people lost everything they owned.

It was now apparent that the land was unsuitable for housing. The remaining houses were pulled down and plans were drawn up to convert the space to a pleasure ground. This was envisaged as 'a park for the working classes' with grand features including glasshouses, a bandstand, a fountain and ornate gates and railings. (Apart from the glasshouses, all these elements are still there today.)

However, the problem remained of how to prevent further slippage. A retaining wall had to be built to prevent the park, and its trees, from falling onto the road beneath, or even onto St Swithin's Church, directly opposite.

Building the wall was no easy task; the first attempt collapsed shortly before the park was officially opened. The final structure – which has fortunately survived the test of time – was designed by T. B. Silcock and completed in 1889.

It is interesting to note that the battlemented tower does not appear in Silcock's original design for the wall. However, the final construction included the tower with battlements and arrow slits that you see today. Perhaps it was a signal that the new wall was intended to be impregnable.

THE TORCHES
OF ST SWITHIN'S MAUSOLEUM

⑱

When time – and money – ran out

Beside St Swithin's Church, The Paragon, BA1 5LY

O ne of Bath's many unfinished projects is St Swithin's Mausoleum. However, one part of the grand design that was completed is the burial place itself, and the wall in front of it, with its curious carvings of upside-down torches.

The Victorian era was a boom time for cemeteries as tombs and graveyards started to become extravagantly ornate. Work on St Swithin's Mausoleum began in the 1830s and the original plan was to have a grand entrance with a school room and a vestry on either side. However, the money ran out and only the mausoleum and the wall were completed.

In the event, the mausoleum was never filled to capacity and the last burial took place in 1860. The building was somewhat neglected and is now blocked off, a large and rather forbidding sight best viewed from the small garden area to the south of the church. (This surprisingly little-visited garden was once a burial place too but is now a peaceful sanctuary with the old gravestones stacked around the sides.)

The mausoleum wall is visible to passers-by. But anyone who stops to look must surely wonder about the four upside-down torches carved into the stone. In fact, these are a form of neoclassical symbolism that was popular at the time although more common in exclusive private cemeteries than in public burial places such as this.

The flame of the torch symbolises life and the immortal soul. But an inverted torch, with the flame leaking out, indicates that – for those behind the wall – time has run out and their earthly existence has been extinguished.

Burials at St Swithin's

Although there are now no visible signs of those who were buried in the mausoleum, St Swithin's is still a rewarding place for the grave-hunter. The church has several very elaborate tombs, including that of the architect John Palmer. And there are two important graves in the churchyard to the north. The first is that of the novelist Fanny Burney and the second is of George Austen. The latter was an Anglican rector and – more famously – the father of Jane Austen.

GAY'S HOUSE ASYLUM SIGN

Where young girls learnt domestic skills

Gay's House, Gay's Hill, BA1 5JN

Bath is full of ghost signs, those painted words and images on the outside of buildings that give a clue to past activities and offer a glimpse of a lost world. One of the most curious of these is on Gay's Hill, where a sign on the side of Gay's House reads, 'Asylum for teaching young females household work'.

The house was not originally intended as an institution. It was built in the late 18th century as a dower house for the influential Rivers-Gay family, who owned the estate of the Manor of Walcot. However, in 1819 the building was converted to an entirely different use.

Following a public meeting at the Guildhall, subscriptions were raised to establish an asylum for 'unprotected females'. In this context, 'asylum' was not pejorative: it was intended to be a training facility and a place of refuge. This was obviously a fashionable cause, with balls and concerts raising substantial donations for it.

The facility was designed for girls between the ages of 12 and 14 who came from poor families or who had no other means of support. They were to be taught needlework and other domestic skills that would prepare them for 'inferior domestic service'.

Despite the best efforts of its patrons, the asylum only operated until 1832, having enjoyed mixed success. Many of its occupants did indeed leave and obtain jobs in service. Others were less fortunate, with some dying of typhus and others being discharged due to ill health. We are also told that three girls were expelled, although their misdeeds are unrecorded, as is their subsequent fate.

If life in the asylum sounds grim, it is worth remembering the likely outcomes for destitute girls who had no means of earning a living. Unless they could find a husband, their options would mostly be limited to the workhouse, crime or prostitution (there was ample demand for the latter in a city with many wealthy visitors).

Gay's House is now a private dwelling again but the asylum sign is still there. It is a reminder of the less glamorous and attractive side of life in the Georgian city.

Ghost signs ... and other clues to the past

The asylum sign on Gay's House (see p. 180) is one of more than 150 ghost signs in and around Bath. But what are ghost signs and why does Bath have so many of them?

Despite the name, there is nothing spooky about these signs. They are merely hand-painted advertisements on old buildings that give a clue to their former use. In some cases, where a building has changed its identity more than once, you may even see one sign painted on top of another.

In the Middle Ages, pubs and other businesses would advertise their existence by hanging signs. These were usually pictorial or symbolic and were an aid to navigation in an age when house numbers did not exist and much of the population was illiterate. However, these signs were banned by the Corporation of Bath in 1766 as part of a series of measures to reduce congestion in the narrow city streets.

Initially the signs were replaced by flat boards on the sides of buildings. But it was soon realised that the local Bath stone was an ideal surface for paint, and signwriters were employed to create advertisements on the outside of commercial premises. These were often eye-catching (a sort of early street art) and designed to be seen at a distance. And now that literacy was less of an issue for urban populations, the signs could incorporate larger amounts of written information.

Walking around Bath, the ghost signs are a reminder of a world that has mostly disappeared. There are signs for 'snuff and tobacco', a circulating library on Milsom Street, and several dairies where householders (or their servants) could buy butter, cream and other fresh goods. Shepherds Hall on Princes Street advertised one of the country's friendly societies, which provided essential health and welfare services in return for a weekly subscription.

In recent years, more attention has been paid to ghost signs and many that were previously painted over have been uncovered. One sign, outside No. 15 Abbey Churchyard, even has its own information plaque.

However, it is not just painted signs that tell you a building was once used for other purposes. Look out for mosaics in door wells, such as the one announcing the Wale clothes shop in George Street (now a lettings agency). And for the ironwork sign above a building in Beauford Square advertising 'J. Ellett, Smith & Plumber'.

You can also find old stained-glass window panels like the ones outside a tile shop in London Road. These show that the premises once offered a dizzying range of goods and services: 'Groceries,

Provisions, Fruits, Post Office, Cereals, Stationery, Confectionery'. Finally, still on London Road, is what seems to be an entire ghost business. Until 2010 what is now the Richer Sounds audiovisual equipment shop was the Porter Butt pub, and much of the original building has been retained. The hanging pub sign (now repainted to say 'Richer Sounds') still bears the golden cockerel symbol of the Courage Brewery. The windows display the words 'Lounge' and 'Public Bar' and on the roof is a carved stone image of a porter butt (historically a container for alcohol).

STATUE OF AESCULAPIUS

⑳

Remains of a lost medical district

Former Bath Ear and Eye Infirmary
W. F. Dolman & Son Funeral Directors, 9 Walcot Terrace, BA1 6AB

Look up as you walk along Walcot Terrace – you might be surprised to spot a rather gloomy-looking stone statue of Aesculapius, the Greco-Roman god of medicine. But what is he doing there and how did he end up above a funeral parlour?

In the early 19th century most of the buildings in Cleveland Place, north of Cleveland Bridge, were associated with the medical profession in one way or another. One of these was the Bath Ear and Eye Infirmary, established in 1837 as a drop-in centre for impoverished citizens. It later moved to grander premises in nearby Walcot Terrace and, although you can no longer get your ears or eyes treated here, you can still see the original exterior.

The hospital relocated to another part of the city in 1914 but the new owners – a funeral business that still trades from the premises – retained the external features, including the doors with their half-glazed windows and the date of 1837 carved into the stonework.

However, the most eye-catching feature is the parapet on top of the building with its statue of Aesculapius. There are several legends associated with him, but one of the most relevant to the Ear and Eye Infirmary is that he was instructed in the arts of healing and medicine by the centaur Chiron.

Unfortunately for Aesculapius, another part of the story is that he was eventually killed by a thunderbolt from Zeus, who was alarmed at the proliferation of human beings caused by Aesculapius' medical knowledge! We can only speculate as to what the god would have thought about the fact that he is now presiding over a firm of undertakers – perhaps that accounts for his glum aspect …

Other traces of a former medical district

When you've had a look at the statue of Aesculapius, walk around the corner to Cleveland Place to see the ghostly remnants of some other medical buildings of the period. The most obvious is the Eastern Dispensary (now home to a rare book dealer) but look closely and you'll also see a sign above the pizza shop that includes the word 'Rheumogen', a one-time patent cure for lumbago and other diseases.

PINCH'S FOLLY

A grand gateway to nowhere

Bathwick Street, outside Henrietta Court, BA2 6PG

As you walk along Bathwick Street you will spot a grand – possibly 19th-century – gateway, built from Bath stone and bearing a coat of arms. Behind it is an undistinguished modern block, but what was there before? A grand manor house, perhaps, or an important public building?

In fact, Pinch's Folly is – as the name implies – no more than a folly, a gateway to nowhere. As far as anyone can tell, it just marked the entrance to a builder's yard owned by John Pinch the Younger. Pinch and his father (John Pinch the Elder) were noted Bath architects and you can see their work around the city, particularly in Bathwick. Yet there is no evidence that either of them intended any type of building to stand on the site behind Pinch's Folly.

The mystery deepens when you realise that the gateway was supposedly erected after both Pinchs had died. And when you look closely you notice that, apart from the scrolls and mouldings that you might expect on a grand entrance, there is a coat of arms on the keystone. These are the arms of Powlett and Lowther, two important local families who would have had no connection with the builder's yard.

This has led to speculation that the gateway is actually much older and that it once led to Bathwick Villa, owned by members of the Powlett and Lowther families. This theory presupposes that it was moved from the villa to the builder's yard, some distance away. But, if so, why would it have been removed some 50 years before the villa was demolished? And why would a 1930s newspaper correspondent have claimed that the arch was built by her grandfather (William Pinch, who owned the yard after the death of his father)?

Whatever the reason, Pinch's Folly remains standing to puzzle passers-by and to liven up an otherwise unremarkable stretch of road.

ST MARY'S CHURCHYARD

An atmospheric graveyard with a ruined chapel

Henrietta Road, BA2 6LY
stmaryschurchyard.com

For many years St Mary's churchyard was one of Bath's closed-off, forgotten places. The first burial took place here in 1808 but by the 1860s the graveyard was full. New cemeteries were built elsewhere and St Mary's was allowed to fall into disrepair. It was eventually closed to the public in 1980, its secrets hidden until a group of volunteers got together to restore and reopen the historic site.

The churchyard reopened in 2006. Paths had been created and memorials repaired. And a lot of work had been done on transcribing the headstones and researching some of the people who were laid to rest here. A trail marking 21 notable graves is now available on the churchyard website.

There is plenty to discover here. There are famous people (like John Pinch the architect) and relatives of the famous (like Sophia Wren, great-granddaughter of Sir Christopher). Some were famous in their time: the tomb of Ellen Pickering reads, 'Author of 16 popular novels. Her greatest success "Nan Darrell or The Gypsy Mother". Died of scarlet fever'. One headstone simply reads 'a loyal servant'; another says – enigmatically – 'a mystery'.

Built into a wall in the corner of the churchyard are the remains of a Roman stone coffin. This is a reminder that the area was used for burying the dead long before the 19th century.

As well as being a pocket of history, St Mary's is also a peaceful retreat. There are trees with nesting boxes, birds and butterflies. And the grass between the graves has been kept in a semi-natural state. Wild flowers abound.

At the centre of the churchyard stands a ruined mortuary chapel. It was built by John Pinch, using stone from the medieval St Mary's Church, demolished in 1818. What you see now is the shell of a building, overshadowed by trees, its roof long gone. Leaves and flowers poke out of every door, window and archway. It is curiously atmospheric. You could easily imagine this as the setting for a Gothic novel.

PENFOLD PILLAR BOX

Rare Victorian postboxes

Outside 51 Great Pulteney Street, BA2 4DP

There are two pillar boxes on Great Pulteney Street: one outside the house at No. 51 and the other at the end of the street in Laura Place. Although their bright red hue makes them instantly recognisable, stop and take a closer look. Not only are they very old, but they have an unusual shape, being hexagonal in form.

Postboxes were introduced to Britain in the mid-19th century by the novelist Anthony Trollope, who worked for the Post Office. Prior to that time, letters either had to be taken to a 'Receiving House' or given to a Bellman, who would walk up and down the streets ringing a bell and collecting the mail. The installation of roadside boxes made posting and collection much easier.

Early designs were in a variety of shapes and colours. The standard red colour was introduced in 1874 as a way of making sure that the boxes could be easily spotted. But it proved much more difficult to agree on the shape and size.

The Post Office wanted a uniform design to cut down on manufacturing costs and in 1866 the architect John Penfold produced a standard model in three sizes. Modifications to the Penfold style were made over the years but they all had some common features. They were hexagonal and topped with decorative caps and finials. And they bore the royal coat of arms and the letters VR, Queen Victoria's monogram.

Although the Penfold postboxes were aesthetically pleasing and popular with the public, they were not practical. Letters could get stuck in the corners or in the cap, sometimes resulting in damage or loss. So the design gradually gave way to the cylindrical boxes that we are familiar with today.

Very few Penfold boxes have survived in Britain. There are perhaps fewer than a hundred left, including these two in Bath.

The box at No. 51 was in danger of removal when its lock wore out. However, it was reprieved when a lockmaker managed to create a copy of the original mechanism. It seems fitting that Penfold's box should still be in use in a city that has such a unique position in postal history.

Bath's place in postal history

In many ways, Bath was central to the development of the British postal service. Two Bath men – Ralph Allen and John Palmer – revolutionised the way that the service was organised. And the city's influence did not end with them …

Ralph Allen (who you will come across many times in this book) was one of the most influential figures in 18th-century Bath. He owned quarries in Combe Down, commissioned the magnificent house and gardens at Prior Park and was a noted philanthropist and one-time mayor of the city.

But all of this was financed from the profits of his first enterprise: the invention of the Cross Post.

Allen first came to Bath as a young man to work for the Post Office, being promoted to postmaster two years later. It was a busy office, handling letters to and from the large number of wealthy visitors who spent long periods in the city every year. However, the service was organised in a remarkably inefficient manner. Strange as it might seem now, all post – even to a nearby destination – was taken to London before being sorted and sent onwards.

The new postmaster came up with the idea of the Cross Post, a seemingly obvious method of creating a cross-country network of mail delivery routes. In 1727 Allen signed a contract with the Post Office to put his ideas into place. This was a gamble on his part as he took some of the financial risk himself. However, it paid off and made him a very rich man. It is also estimated that the Cross Post saved the Post Office around £1.5m over the next 40 years.

The next innovation came from John Palmer. Not to be confused with the Bath architect of the same name, Palmer was the son of a brewer who also owned a theatre in Old Orchard Street (now the Masonic Museum – see p. 48). He was instrumental in gaining a royal warrant for the theatre and later established a second theatre in Bristol.

Palmer used strongly guarded night coaches to move people, scenery and props between his two theatres. He soon realised that a similar scheme could be used for the mail, which was at that time transported across the country by mounted carriers. Despite a certain amount of opposition, he was able to introduce a mail coach system which facilitated a quicker, safer and cheaper delivery of letters and valuables.

There are other connections between Bath and postal history. The world's first postage stamp – the Penny Black – was first used on a letter with a Bath postmark.

The idea of pre-paid stamps was introduced by Rowland Hill, a social campaigner, and the first stamp was due to be issued on 6 May 1840. However, whether by accident or design, Thomas Moore Musgrave, the Bath postmaster of the time, used a stamp on a letter to a family member on 2 May.

And, finally, when the trademark red colour was adopted for postboxes, the job of repainting the existing boxes went to a Bath firm. That same firm was responsible for painting all new postboxes for many decades.

Until 2023 the story of Bath's postal history was told in the small but interesting Postal Museum. It is hoped that its exhibits will eventually be displayed in other museums around the city. In the meantime, a plaque outside the old Post Office celebrates the achievements of Ralph Allen and John Palmer.

VELLORE HOUSE GROTTO

A 19th-century folly

In the grounds of Bath Spa Hotel
Sydney Road, BA2 6NS
macdonaldhotels.co.uk/bath
Bus 11 from Guildhall to Darlington Road

The Bath Spa Hotel is situated in a Gothic Revival mansion with classically styled grounds. A particular feature of the gardens is the grotto, a romantic folly whose origins are shrouded in mystery.

The mansion was built in 1835 for Colonel Augustus Andrews, who named it Vellore House after the garrison town of Vellore, in India, where he had been stationed. Following the colonel's death, this large and magnificent building was variously used as a hospital and a nurses' home before being transformed into a luxury hotel. Over the years, it has hosted visitors as diverse as Winston Churchill, Joan Collins and Emperor Haile Selassie (who later lived in Fairfield House, see p. 152).

Colonel Andrews obviously intended to enjoy his new home, because it was set in 3 hectares of carefully designed gardens, with conservatories, hothouses and several specimen trees. There was a small Greek-style temple, and the grotto was added shortly before the colonel's death in 1858.

Built of rough local limestone and tufa rock, the semicircular structure is formed of a central cave surrounded by arches and a pathway. The central area opens up to a skylight, perhaps prompting the statement that this was 'a place where in the summer heat the most delicious quietude and repose may be enjoyed'. Unfortunately, the inner cave is now closed off, but you can still walk around the outside of the grotto.

The mystery (if there is one) surrounds the grotto's origins. We are told that the colonel paid £1,000 to build it, the suggestion being that it was newly constructed at that time. However, the material and style are much more in keeping with the fashion of the 18th century than of the 1850s.

Furthermore, we know that there was once a very similar grotto in nearby Sydney Gardens, removed around 1853. There is no record of what happened to it – could it have been acquired by Colonel Andrews and re-sited in the grounds of Vellore House?

ALICE PARK WILDLIFE GARDEN

A hidden nature reserve

Alice Park, Gloucester Road, BA1 7BL
alicepark.co.uk
Bus 7 from Guildhall to Larkhall, then 8-min. walk

Alice Park is very much a community space, with sports facilities, large grassy areas and a popular cafe. There are all sorts of things to discover here, including (hidden at the back of the park) a small wildlife garden and pond.

The park was created in 1938 from land donated by Herbert Montgomery MacVicar in memory of his wife Alice. It was to be an amenity area for the local people, with an emphasis on children and team sports. Today a cycle track and a skate park take their place alongside a playground and tennis courts. And the park is used for everything from fitness classes to youth football to neighbourhood events.

With its open spaces, paths and trees, Alice Park is also a place to walk and unwind. But if you really want to escape the crowds and find some peace and quiet, the wildlife garden is the place to go. The centrepiece of the garden is the well-established lily pool, which – according to a plaque beside the water – was created as a memorial to Alice MacVicar's brother-in-law, a veteran of the First World War who died in 1937.

Visiting in the spring, I saw numerous tadpoles and water boatmen, lily pads and irises. But the pond is also home to koi carp, dragonflies and newts. Of course all those tadpoles will later become frogs and toads, who will disappear into the undergrowth before reappearing for next year's breeding season. Perhaps inevitably – given the availability of fish and frogs – herons are sometimes seen here. And foxes and badgers are frequent visitors.

Around the pond is a grassy area, and behind the trees a hidden path encircles the garden. Rewilding of the garden began a few years ago and the long-term aim is to create a wild-flower meadow to attract bees and other wildlife.

Although it is partly the responsibility of the local council, the wildlife garden is largely a labour of love by enthusiastic local volunteers. Like all the best gardens, it is very much a work in progress.

CHEQUERBOARD
AT THE BLADUD'S HEAD

A mysterious sign on the side of a pub

Bladud's Head, 1 Catsley Place, Larkhall, BA1 6TA
Bus 7 from Guildhall to Linen Walk

Walk to the end of St Saviour's Road in Larkhall, where the city meets the country, and you'll come to the Bladud's Head. Before you go inside for a welcome drink, stop to look at the signs painted on the outside wall.

First you'll notice the ghost sign – probably originally painted in the 19th century – telling us that the pub is licensed to sell 'beer ale porter cyder & tobacco'. Then you'll see the rather more unusual sign beside it, a chequerboard with red and blue squares wrapped around the corner of the wall. But what does it signify and why is it there?

There is nothing obvious in the pub's history to give us a clue. Originally part of a row of three late 18th-century houses, it opened as a pub in the 1840s. Another pub, the Wagon & Horses, opened next door in the 1870s but was taken over by the Bladud's Head in 1890.

The pub was at one time threatened with closure but has since been reprieved and is now a thriving local. It was during renovation work in 2013 that the signs on the wall were rediscovered and repainted.

At one time, 'The Chequers' was the most common name for a pub in England. It seems that the ubiquity of the name led to the chequerboard becoming synonymous with pubs: it is said to go back to the Romans, with similar signs having been found on houses in Pompeii. So the painted sign might simply have existed to alert illiterate travellers to the fact that this was a tavern.

Other theories exist. The chequerboard is known to be a Masonic symbol (see p. 42). Perhaps this was a sign that Freemasons were welcome here or even that this was a regular place for Masons' meetings.

A more recent suggestion is that the pattern was a warning to anyone approaching that they were in danger of hitting their head on the corner of the wall. Although such a warning might have been more necessary for those leaving the pub after a hard night's drinking than for those on their way in!

Rolling down the stone head of King Bladud

You might think that the stone head of King Bladud above the door is the origin of the pub's name. However, locals will tell you that this head originally stood outside the Bladud's Arms, around the corner on Gloucester Road. When this pub closed, the head was rolled down the hill to its new home!

BAILBROOK MISSION CHURCH

A prefabricated Victorian church

113 Bailbrook Lane, BA1 7AL
Bus 3 from Hilton Hotel to Bailbrook House

If you walk along the quiet Bailbrook Lane, with its stone cottages and panoramic views, you might be surprised to see a disused church fashioned from corrugated metal. This was once the Bailbrook Mission Church, built for local workers in 1892.

Many new churches were built in England in the 19th century. This was partly in response to a population shift from the countryside to cities caused by the Industrial Revolution, and partly to combat a decline in Church of England congregations. Many of these new churches were ornate and expensively furnished, such as St Stephen's on Lansdown Road (see p. 171). At the other end of the scale were simple prefabricated constructions, designed to be put up in a hurry and removed when no longer required.

Corrugated iron was invented in 1829 and allowed for the construction of prefabricated buildings, including churches. Several different designs were created and manufacturers produced catalogues of the available choices.

Known as 'tin tabernacles', many of these churches were built between the 1850s and the early 20th century. They were mostly in semi-rural or working-class areas and were usually intended to be temporary. Fewer than 100 remain across the country today.

The Bailbrook Mission Church was built for workers at the local Robertson's jam factory. It was the most expensive church in the catalogue of William Cooper of London and was unusually elaborate for this type of structure.

The church is built with a timber frame covered in corrugated iron. Despite the material, it has many of the features you would expect of a Gothic church, including a tower, large arched windows and doorways, and stained glass. Inside it was fitted with a pulpit and pews.

The Mission Church was converted into a private house in 1991 and was known locally as 'Our Lady of Crinkly Tins'. It later fell into disrepair. Today the structure is intact but damaged in places and surrounded by vegetation.

The good news is that the church has recently been sold and that the new owners plan to renovate it and to restore the interior as a home. So passers-by will once again be able to see the Bailbrook Mission Church as it would have looked in Victorian times.

LITTLE SOLSBURY HILL MAZE

A labyrinth built during a road-building protest

Little Solsbury Hill, Batheaston, BA1 7JQ
Bus 231 from Guildhall to Vale View Terrace, then 25-min. walk
Parking available in Batheaston, then follow footpath up the hill

Little Solsbury Hill is one of the seven hills surrounding Bath. It was once topped by an Iron Age fort, but in more recent times it has

been prized as a beauty spot with walks and spectacular views. It was also the subject of a well-known 1977 song by Peter Gabriel, who lived in the area for many years.

This peaceful landscape was threatened in the 1990s when a bypass to the nearby A46 was being planned. Alarmed at the news that the new road would run along the side of the hill, protesters immediately set up camp and tried to disrupt the construction. Supporters of the protest arrived from across the country, followed by alarming reports of people being beaten by security guards, resulting in a number of hospitalisations.

Despite the violence, the protesters stayed in their camp for some months. During this time they managed to carve a seven-circuit labyrinth in the grass, in a spot overlooking the road-building site. Curiously, no one now seems to remember whose idea it was or why they chose a labyrinth as their symbol. However, the protest apparently 'identified with the Celts', harking back to earlier times. So perhaps the idea of a labyrinth (which goes back to antiquity) was appropriate.

In the end, the protest was unsuccessful and the road was completed in 1996, neatly cutting the hill in half. However, Little Solsbury Hill remains a popular place for walks, picnics and sunset views. And the labyrinth is still there, the only reminder of a turbulent interlude.

For more information about mazes and labyrinths, see following page.

Labyrinth in St John the Baptist Church, Batheaston

Another modern labyrinth can be found in the nearby church of St John the Baptist in Batheaston. The church suffered an arson attack in 1986, necessitating a substantial restoration of the interior. The then vicar, Paul Lucas, took the opportunity to design and build a stone floor maze in part of the church.

This maze is a copy of a 13th-century design from the abbey of St Omer in France. It features a grid of 49 x 49 squares, and symbologists will tell you that the square of 7 has particular mystical significance, connected with the goddess Venus. However, there is no evidence that the monks of St Omer chose the design for its pagan associations!

Mazes and labyrinths

The maze on Little Solsbury Hill is modern, but at one time turf mazes were a common feature of the English countryside. In the Middle Ages at least 60 were known to have existed in England and there were many others across northern Europe.

Mazes have ancient origins and appear in all mythologies. In the western tradition, they recall the Minotaur of Crete and the labyrinthine walls of Troy. Indeed, some English mazes had names like 'City of Troy' or 'Julian's Bower' (thought to be a reference to Julius, son of Aeneas, who introduced Roman mazes to the city of Troy).

Maze designs started to appear in churches in the Middle Ages, a famous example being the one in Chartres Cathedral in France. And they were built in the countryside, most often cut into grass but sometimes constructed from stones (as in some remaining mazes in Scandinavia and in the Scilly Isles in Cornwall).

Strictly speaking, these are labyrinths rather than mazes. Although there were different designs, they were all unicursal, with just one path to the centre and no false turns. This differentiates them from the later 'puzzle mazes' in which it is easy to get lost on the way to the middle.

There is much debate as to what these early mazes were actually for although it seems that they performed a mixed religious and social function. The common feature of all labyrinths is that their paths are winding and that they are very long compared with the actual distance from the entrance to the centre. This is supposed to represent the journey of the soul: the goal is clear but there are twists and turns on the way to achieving it.

Labyrinths were also linked with the idea of pilgrimage. For many people – limited by time or money or just not permitted to leave their village – an actual pilgrimage was impossible. But they could walk, or sometimes crawl on their knees, around the paths of a labyrinth, stopping for reflection or prayer at each turn.

In some cases, such a 'pilgrimage' could be imposed upon a sinner as a penance. A further possibility is that mazes were used as a way to trap the Devil, or other evil spirits, who could only travel in straight lines.

Whatever the religious purpose of labyrinths, we know that they also played a part in community life. Maze games were popular, particularly during village fairs and festivals. These were usually connected with courtship and fertility rituals, and there are stories of the proceedings becoming quite lively!

There may have been some conflict between the religious and social aspects of labyrinths, as Oliver Cromwell banned maze games during the Commonwealth of 1649–60. However, they were soon revived and persisted into the 19th century.

Turf labyrinths need regular recutting if they are to survive and today only eight medieval mazes remain in England. However, there has been a recent revival of interest in labyrinths and some new mazes have been created, including some cut from turf (like the one on Little Solsbury Hill).

Most modern mazes, whether made from turf or other materials, are created as artworks rather than for religious purposes. An example of this is the Beazer Maze near Pulteney Bridge (see p. 104).

© Rolf Kranz

CHILCOMBE BOTTOM

One of the best wildlife areas in the region

Batheaston, BA1 8EL
Bus 3 from Guildhall to Vale View Terrace, then 28-min. walk

At the bottom of a deep valley behind Batheaston is a small nature reserve that is home to hundreds of native plants and animals. Created on the site of a former reservoir, Chilcombe Bottom is one of the best wildlife areas in the region. It is also a piece of social history, a reminder of early efforts to bring water to the people of Bath.

In Victorian times there was enormous pressure to improve sanitation. Amongst other measures this necessitated the provision of a fresh water supply. The Batheaston Reservoir opened in 1848, taking advantage of the abundant springs in the valley between Charmy Down and Little Solsbury Hill. It remained in use until the 1980s.

In 1995 the site – now owned by Wessex Water – was turned into a nature reserve. Streams and ponds were created, and hedges and trees were planted. And – as a way of preserving a bit of the site's history – some of the structures associated with the waterworks were retained. A small valve house sits outside the gate and you can still hear the water rushing beneath the nearby well.

The ponds and surrounding grassland are home to a massive variety of plants, and this in turn encourages a wide range of animal life. It is estimated that more than 400 types of invertebrates live here, including some rare species. There are also birds and frogs, and you may even be lucky enough to spot an adder in the grass.

In some ways, this feels more like a place for animals than for humans: as Chilcombe Bottom is so hidden away, you're unlikely to encounter many other people. There are no facilities for visitors other than an information board, but this does mean that you can enjoy the natural setting without distraction (if you want a seat, you'll have to try the mossy top of the well …).

You can walk to Chilcombe Bottom from Batheaston or from the Swainswick layby on the A46. Either way, remember that it's at the bottom of a valley and there will be some hills involved!

CHARMY DOWN AIRFIELD

A wartime airbase

Charmy Down, BA1 8AG
Bus X79 to Charmy Down, then 25-min. walk

Charmy Down is a quiet plateau to the north of Bath, separated from Little Solsbury Hill by the equally remote Chilcombe Bottom (see p. 206). But it was not always so peaceful; during the Second World War it was home to fighter aircraft.

In 1941 the RAF built a military airfield on Charmy Down, flattening a prehistoric burial site in the process. There were three runways, 12 aircraft hangars and several support buildings. The base was initially a home for Hawker Hurricane jets, which were painted black so that they could fly at night. This enabled them to intercept enemy aircraft on their way to bombing raids on Bath and Bristol.

In 1943 the airfield was taken over by the US Air Force, which stationed a variety of fighter jets here. After the war, it was briefly used by the Air Training Corps, but it finally closed in 1946.

Part of the old airfield is now accessible via a public footpath which follows the line of what would have been a runway although it is now a farm track. As you walk up here, it's easy to see why the site was chosen by the RAF. It's a large upland expanse in a hilly area where flat land is a bit of a rarity. And it has excellent visibility in all directions.

A memorial stone commemorates the area's wartime activities. And fragments of the past remain: a few pillboxes are still visible, as are the entrances to underground ammunition stores and the remains of a gun-testing area.

Charmy Down has now reverted to farmland use, and an attempt to convert it to a Park and Ride in 2008 was rejected. The only recent event to shatter the peace was an illegal rave in 2020 that attracted 3,000 revellers and kept the locals awake all night.

If you make the trek up to Charmy Down today, you're unlikely to encounter anything noisier than a tractor or a herd of cows …

ST CATHERINE'S CHURCH

A hidden church in the grounds of a private house

Batheaston, BA1 8HA
Open during daylight hours
Sunday services twice a month
Bus X31 from Guildhall to Vale View Terrace, then 42-min. walk

The church of St Catherine, in the parish of St Catherine's near Batheaston, is very small, but it probably doesn't need to be larger because the community it serves is tiny. It isn't particularly easy to get to as it's hidden in the grounds of a private house.

St Catherine's has acted as a parish church since 1258, when – together with the adjoining estate – it was given to Bath Abbey. But since the church is in the grounds of St Catherine's Court, its history has followed the whims and fortunes of the inhabitants of the mansion house.

The church was substantially rebuilt in 1490, the tower was reconstructed in 1704 and the interior was given a full make-over in the mid-19th century. Inside the church are family tombs and memorials from the earliest times to the 20th century.

Those who make the effort to visit St Catherine's will be rewarded by a very fine interior with elements from different eras such as a 12th-century font and a 15th-century pulpit. There are remnants of medieval glass and an unusual 'squint' (a small opening allowing a view of the altar) in the wall behind the vicar's stall.

Particularly remarkable is the Victorian tilework. Painted tiles and mosaics cover the tower and chancel arches. Some are purely decorative; others spell out the Creed and the Ten Commandments.

Before leaving, stand outside the church and look up at the south side of the tower. On one side of the window at the top is a sundial; on the other is an inscription commemorating the 1704 rebuilding.

St Catherine's is 3 km north of Batheaston. You can walk or drive, but if you choose to drive, be aware that the lane is extremely narrow.

Although there's no public access to St Catherine's Court, you will see the house as you approach the church. There was a Benedictine foundation here as far back as 950 but the current grand house and gardens date from the Tudor era. It is now a luxury residence available for private hire.

SUFFRAGETTE MEMORIAL

A reminder of Batheaston's safe house for suffragettes

Outside Eagle House, Northend, Batheaston, BA1 7EH
Bus 3 from Guildhall to Vale View Terrace, then 15-min. walk

Walking past Eagle House in Batheaston, you'll see an old telephone box with the words 'Suffragette Memorial' written across the top. This is a celebration of the role played by the house in the struggle for women's suffrage at the beginning of the 20th century.

Before the First World War, Eagle House was owned by Emily Blathwayt, a member of the Women's Social and Political Union (WSPU), and her husband, Colonel Linley Blathwayt. Between 1909 and 1912 they offered sanctuary to suffragettes following their release from prison, and the house became known as 'Suffragette's Rest' or 'Suffragette's Retreat'.

Many of the women who came here had been treated very roughly in prison, in some cases having been brutally force-fed when they went on hunger strike. Others were simply exhausted from prolonged campaigning. In all cases, the opportunity to recuperate in a sympathetic house with a large garden must have been very welcome.

Prominent visitors included Emmeline and Christabel Pankhurst, and Annie Kenney, the Bristol WPSU organiser. However, the Brathwayts later distanced themselves from the more violent activities of the suffragette movement. Some of the more disruptive members were even barred from Eagle House.

Even in the early days, it was felt that some sort of memorial was needed for those who had fought so hard for women's suffrage. From 1909 trees were planted in what became known as 'Annie's Arboretum' (named after Annie Kenney). Each tree represented a woman who had been imprisoned or been on hunger strike.

Unfortunately the arboretum was destroyed in the 1960s to make way for a new housing estate. Just one tree survived, now in the private garden of Eagle House. So a more permanent memorial was required.

In 2022 the local council funded the conversion of a disused phone box to commemorate Batheaston's role in the campaign for votes for women. The box is now painted in the suffragette colours of purple, green and white, with ribbons of the same colours on the door handle. These are symbolic of the core suffragette values: purple for loyalty and dignity, white for purity and green for hope.

BATHEASTON SECRET GARDEN

A historic walled garden beside the river

Stambridge, Batheaston, BA1 7NB
Bus 3 from Guildhall to Stambridge

Until the 1990s the Secret Garden in Batheaston was so secret that there was no way through the high wall surrounding it. Even now, despite its public access and riverside location, it remains quiet and secluded, a peaceful retreat on a sunny afternoon.

The garden was built as part of the adjoining Batheaston House in 1712. It was a private area with walls on two sides, the other sides bounded by the house and the river. It was laid out formally with paths and with a shell niche seat built into one wall.

In 1959 the garden was separated from the house and it gradually fell into disrepair. It was later acquired by the local council and opened to the public in 1991. But only in the last few years has it started to take its current form, thanks to the hard work of a team of volunteers.

The layout of the garden is now much as it might have been in the 18th century. The original walls and the shell niche remain, the only major change being the two gateways built into the east wall. A particular feature of these gateways is the series of modern carvings around the edges.

The Secret Garden is planted with trees, shrubs and flowerbeds. The oldest tree is a mulberry, said to be well over a hundred years old. The garden is criss-crossed with paths, creating a number of hidden areas. And there are seats where you can sit and enjoy the calm.

At the far side of the garden is a new Forest Garden area. This community project is attempting to recreate the ecosystem of a natural woodland. In the longer term, it will include a variety of useful plants – edible, medicinal and industrial.

The Forest Garden is a work in progress but it already seems to be paying dividends. A noticeboard displays some of the wildlife that can be spotted here, with an impressive range of butterflies and beetles.

BATHEASTON WATERWHEEL

A new use for old technology

Beside the Old Mill Hotel
Toll Bridge Road, Batheaston, BA1 7DE
Bus 3 from Guildhall to Clarence Gardens

At one time there were around 30 water mills on the River Avon between Bath and Bristol. These have now mostly disappeared, although you can still see the remains of Monk's Mill in the centre of Bath. But an ambitious new scheme has breathed new life into the Batheaston waterwheel, allowing it to generate electricity for the adjacent hotel.

Water power has been in use for 2,000 years, since the Chinese used it to process grain. By the Middle Ages there were thousands of water mills grinding corn in England. Many more mills were built during the Industrial Revolution to support the growth of the cotton industry. However, the availability of different sources of energy, such as coal and oil, gradually made the old water wheels redundant.

At least three mills are known to have existed in the Batheaston area. The first recorded mention of the flour mill on the river between Batheaston and Bathampton is in the 1500s, but it may go back as far as Norman times. During the 19th century there was also a brewery here, but operations ceased after a fire in 1909. A hotel and restaurant were later built on the site.

The old waterwheel was replaced by a decorative version in 1987. However, concerns about the use of fossil fuels and a drive for cleaner energy led to calls to consider generating electricity from the water. A new waterwheel was installed in 2016.

The wheel now runs for 24 hours a day. It's only turned off if the water level becomes too high or too low or if a hotel guest asks for it to be paused. It has the capacity to generate 13.5 kW of electricity, the equivalent of that used by 20 homes in a year. It currently provides a substantial proportion of the energy used by the hotel and restaurant.

The waterwheel is also intended to be a local attraction and there is an information board in the meadows on the opposite side of the river. You can see the wheel from here or from the road outside the hotel. Alternatively you can sit on the terrace of the Old Mill restaurant and enjoy a drink while listening to the chugging of the wheel and the swishing of the water.

BATHEASTON TOLL BRIDGE

A historic river crossing

Toll Bridge Road, Batheaston, BA1 7DE
Bus 3 from Guildhall to Clarence Gardens
Small charge for vehicles using the river crossing

Batheaston Toll Bridge
List of Tolls
All Charges Are Each Way

Persons Walking Weekly	6d
Motor Lorries, Cattle Trucks, etc.	1'
Tractors 1 ton and over	6d
Small Tractors, Landrovers, Pick-ups etc	6d
Vans under 1 ton	6d
Carriages Drawn by One Horse	3d
Including Return Journey	4d
By Two Horses	4d
By Three Horses	6d
Cycle for Two	2d
Cycles, Truck, Wheelbarrow	1d
Perambulator or Mailcart	1d
Motor Cycles With Pillion	2d
Motor Side Cars	1d
Small Trailer Drawn by Car	4d
Large Trailer	1'
Private Cars	6d
Dormobiles	6d
" " Over 4 Passengers	1'
Person Riding on Horseback	2d
Cattle per Head	½d
Sheep or Pigs per Score	6d
Donkey and Cart	3d
Wheelchair Drawn by Hand	2d
Wheelchair Drawn by Donkey or Pony	3d

In the past, crossing a river could be a costly business, payment being made to a ferryman or a toll keeper at the side of a bridge. One place where the tradition of paying to go over the water still survives is at the Batheaston Toll Bridge, which crosses the River Avon to the east of Bath.

Bridges (as well as roads) were often built using private money and it was natural that the owners would wish to recoup their investment by levying a small charge on those who used the bridge. Bath is surrounded by a river on three sides and had many such crossings, designed to facilitate journeys to and from the city.

Today tolls are more likely to be levied on modern roads and bridges but there are a few historic survivors. The Batheaston Toll Bridge is one of these and charges the princely sum of £1 for cars crossing the river to Bathampton (although season tickets are available).

The river was originally traversed by a horse ferry. But in 1870 the Bridge Company Turnpike Trust built the current bridge, an attractive structure with three central arches and smaller arches on either side.

A board by the side of the bridge – sometimes also known as the Bathampton Bridge – shows an old list of toll charges. A reference to 'motor lorries' suggests that these are not the 1870 prices but the list does give us some clue as to what the crossing must once have looked like.

We are told that 'persons walking' would be charged ½d and 'carriages drawn by one horse' 3d. There is a long list of other potential traffic, including tractors, wheelbarrows, cattle and sheep. Any modern-day user will know that the bridge is narrow and can sometimes get congested. Just imagine the chaos that must have ensued a hundred years ago with such a huge mixture of humans, animals and mechanised vehicles!

The 10th most profitable toll in England

Why does the Batheaston Bridge continue to charge a toll? The answer is simply that it is still privately owned. And in 2022 it was reported to be the 10th most profitable toll in England.

KANGAROOS IN
A STAINED-GLASS WINDOW

Kangaroos, convicts and the settlement of Australia

Australia Chapel, St Nicholas Church, Bathampton, BA2 6TU
stnicholasbathampton.org.uk
Bus 11 from Guildhall to Down Lane Bottom, then 5-min. walk

The Church of St Nicholas in Bathampton is possibly the only place you'll ever see kangaroos in a stained-glass window. In fact, the whole church has an Australian feel, with a chapel dedicated to the former colony and even a small exhibition area.

The connection between Bath and Australia starts to make sense when you discover that this is the burial place of Admiral Arthur Phillip. He was the first governor of New South Wales and the founder of modern Australia. In 1788 he sailed into Botany Bay with a fleet of ships carrying convicts and set about building the new settlement.

It wasn't until 1974 that the admiral's burial place got the recognition it deserved and a part of the church was rededicated as the Australia Chapel. Built with assistance from the Australian government, it is a celebration of all things Australian, with wood and marble specially transported from down under. The windows of the chapel show the crests of the federal government and of each individual state. This is where the kangaroos come in.

At the other end of the church, information boards tell the story of Arthur Phillip and the settlement of Australia. Of particular interest is a list of the names of the 'First Fleeters', showing in each case the place of sentencing and the length of their term. (In most cases, the sentence was either seven years or life – given the near impossibility of ever returning to England, there would have been little practical difference between the two.)

By now you might be wondering how Arthur Phillip came to be buried in Bathampton. The answer is that – unlike his unfortunate human cargo – he had no difficulty in returning to England after a few years and eventually he retired to Bath for the benefit of his health. His tomb is here and once a year, in October, the High Commissioner for Australia performs a wreath-laying ceremony.

But that is not quite the end of the story, as there have since been calls for Arthur Phillip's remains to be returned to Australia.

ELSIE ADELINE LUKE'S GRAVE ㊲

The Bathampton mystery

St Nicholas Church, Bathampton, BA2 6TU
Bus 11 from Guildhall to Down Lane Bottom, then 5-min. walk

Here
lie the remains
of
ELSIE ADELINE LUKE
aged 26
Who was cruelly murdered
on Hampton Down
1 August 1891

A plain tombstone in the corner of St Nicholas churchyard in Bathampton may not immediately catch the eye. But stop to read the inscription and you'll realise that there is a story behind the stone. Delve deeper and you'll find that it's a story shrouded in mystery.

The wording on the stone reads: 'Here lie the remains of ELSIE ADELINE LUKE aged 26, Who was cruelly murdered on Hampton Down, August 1891'. You might wonder why it was necessary to say 'cruelly' – could murder ever be otherwise? – and about the circumstances in which Elsie met her end. This will lead you to the 'Bathampton mystery', a notorious case that aroused a great deal of public interest.

The story begins in 1893, when two boys walking on Bathampton Down found the remains of a body in a cave. It was assumed to be that of Elsie Adeline Luke, who had vanished two years earlier. Her disappearance attracted little comment at the time; she had just lost her job as a cook and was said to be both dishonest and unpopular with her fellow servants.

Even after two years, it was obvious from Elsie's body that she had been murdered. Suspicion immediately fell upon Arthur Stephenson Coombs, an apprentice coach builder who had been 'keeping company' with Elsie prior to her disappearance. The case against him deepened when it was revealed that Elsie had claimed to be pregnant.

Unsurprisingly, Arthur denied the charge. The evidence against him was purely circumstantial and the jury at his trial decided to acquit him. No further investigation was undertaken. Perhaps, given the social attitudes of the era, it was felt that enough time and money had been spent on the murder of a young woman of dubious reputation.

However, there were some who felt that Elsie should have a proper memorial. A local surgeon raised £5 to pay for a headstone in Bathampton. And when that stone crumbled, a replacement was funded from the estate of Lucy Barlow, a well-known local golfer who left money to the village to finance local history projects. Elsie's life may have been short but she is not forgotten.

BOX ROCK CIRCUS

An educational tool, travelling back in time

Valens Terrace, Box, SN13 8NT
boxrockcircus.org.uk
Bus X31 from the Guildhall to Box pharmacy; or drive and park outside
Selwyn Hall

Unlike the more famous stone circles in this part of the country, Box Rock Circus is neither large nor prehistoric. And unlike Stonehenge or Avebury, we know exactly when the rock circus was built and what it is for. It might even be modern … but that doesn't stop it claiming to take visitors back more than 400 million years.

Historically, there were several quarries in and around the village of Box and the area was known for its Box Ground Stone. The last quarry closed in the 1950s but extraction started up again in 2011. The Rock Circus was built the following year, a commemoration of the region's links with stone and quarrying.

The ring of stones is primarily an educational tool to teach children (and interested adults) about Britain's geological history. It is designed to showcase a range of rocks, minerals and fossils and to encourage visitors to think about the make-up and evolution of the Earth.

The Box Rock Circus manages to pack a lot of ideas into a small space. The circle consists of eight blocks of stone, including an obelisk made of the local limestone. Two of the stones are climbing blocks (yes, young visitors are encouraged to be tactile!), made up of different rocks and minerals. And the Fossil Rubbing Block is covered with casts of real fossils – if you come armed with paper and pencils, you can take rubbings from them.

The circus is surrounded by a timeline with black and red marks indicating key dates in the Earth's history. And there are dinosaur footprints in between the stones …

An interpretation board explains the different stones and the timeline. And if you want to go into more detail, you can go online and look at the site's Earthcache (a bit like a geocache but more scientific). Here you will find lots of questions and discussion points based around the stones.

CHAPEL PLAISTER

A medieval pilgrims' chapel

Bradford Road, Box, SN13 8HZ
achurchnearyou.com/church/11757
Open for Sunday services; and Wed 2pm–4pm May to Sept (check website for details)
Car parking beside the chapel

The Pilgrims' Chapel at Chapel Plaister is one of Britain's smallest churches, almost unknown to anyone outside its congregation of around 20 people. But it would once have been familiar to pilgrims looking for a place to spend the night; it is one of just a handful of pilgrimage refuges still in existence.

The first written record of the chapel is dated 1340. Today it stands on a quiet road with few passers-by, but in the 14th century this was the main road to the south-west, a route frequented by pilgrims journeying to Glastonbury to visit the shrine of Joseph of Arimathea.

In those days, pilgrims would travel with their families and all their worldly belongings, including their cattle. The building originally had two storeys with an outside spiral staircase, an arrangement that allowed the men to sleep downstairs and the woman upstairs, while there was space outside for the cattle to graze. In reality, there was little sleeping done as religious services were conducted throughout the night (the upper floor was open at one end so that the women could watch the proceedings).

After the Reformation, the chapel was converted to various uses, including a beer cellar, a bakery and a private house. Its most famous resident was a notorious highwayman. It became a church again in 1893 and was fully restored in 1999.

Today services are held at Chapel Plaister on Sundays and at Christmas. It is also open to visitors on Wednesday afternoons in the summer. A helpful volunteer will be on hand to explain the history and to point out some of the interesting architectural details.

As you enter, look for the stone scallop shell above the door. This symbol was commonly used in the Middle Ages to indicate an overnight shelter for pilgrims and to reassure them they were on the right road.

THE PINNACLE

An unusual pyramidical tomb to stop the deceased's wife dancing on his grave!

Churchyard of St Thomas à Becket Church
Church Lane, Box, SN13 8NR
Bus X31 from Guildhall to Box Pharmacy

The churchyard of St Thomas à Becket Church in Box is full of large and impressive chest tombs. But, tucked away in a gloomy corner, is a rather more unusual grave. It bears no markings and has a slightly unconventional form: it is in the shape of a pyramid.

Although uncommon, the pyramid design is not unique and a few other examples can be found in English churchyards. In some cases, this shape may have resulted from the 'Egyptomania' sweeping the country in the 18th and 19th centuries, or it might just have been an individual eccentricity.

However, more mystical theories exist. Pyramids could be seen as a way of confounding the Devil or, conversely, of aiding the soul on its way to heaven.

Little is known about the pyramid in St Thomas à Becket churchyard, known locally as The Pinnacle. It has been suggested that it is the grave of a man who lived in the nearby house known as The Hermitage at some time in the Georgian era, but this is unproven. The fact that the grave is unmarked, and that it is situated on a shady side of the churchyard, suggests that its occupant was less wealthy or of lower status than those in the larger and showier tombs round about.

But while the identity of the deceased is unknown, everyone seems to be clear about the purpose of the pyramid … and it has nothing to do with demons, or souls, or even the Egyptians. According to local legend, the man was on unfriendly terms with his wife and he wanted to make sure that she could not dance on his grave after his death!

The church of St Thomas à Becket may have ancient origins, being close to the site of a former Roman villa. What you see today dates from the 12th century and it was probably dedicated to St Thomas because it stood on the Pilgrims' Way leading to Canterbury.

You may notice that some of the larger tombs in the churchyard are starting to sink into the ground. This is not surprising, as spring water runs beneath the graves; you can see the springs rising up in the neighbouring garden.

BROWNE'S FOLLY

A tower without a purpose

Monkton Fairleigh, BA1 7TW
Car park on Prospect Place; a footpath leads up the hill

Y ou can see Browne's Folly on the hilltop from many places around the city, but you might wonder what it is and what it was for. It was built in 1845 by Colonel Wade Browne, a quarry owner and the squire of Monkton Farleigh Manor. However, he left no record as to the reason for its construction and we are left to speculate about his motives.

What we do know is that the tower was built during a period of rural depression. One theory is that Browne hoped to create a prominent advertisement for the stone from his quarries. Another is that he wanted to create work for unemployed labourers. Either way, the tower was built, commanding spectacular views of the surrounding countryside.

At the beginning of the 20th century, Browne's Folly was acquired by Sir Charles Hobhouse. He restored the tower in 1907 and it became a meeting place for his shooting parties.

The site is now owned by the Avon Wildlife Trust and the tower has become the focal point of the Browne's Folly nature reserve. Sloping down towards the River Avon, and built on the site of the former quarries, the reserve is a flower-rich area of woods and grassland with a number of walking trails. It has been designated a Site of Special Scientific Interest because of its varied plant life and geological importance.

The square tower stands approximately 12 metres high, with a spiral staircase around the inner edge. You can go inside at any time but there is no handrail … However, you can enjoy the views and the nature reserve just as well from the bottom.

To get to the tower, park in the car park at the bottom of the hill and walk up to the top. Note that the paths are steep and can get muddy in the winter.

You may notice that the tower is sometimes referred to as Brown's Folly. However, Wade Browne himself always spelt his name with an 'e'.

ARTEFACTS AT
THE QUARRYMAN'S ARMS

A piece of quarrying history

Box Hill, Corsham, SN13 8HN
butcombe.com/the-quarrymans-arms-wiltshire
Bus X31 from Guildhall to Hedgesparrow Lane

Today the Quarryman's Arms in Box is a country pub with rooms, excellent food and magnificent views across the valley towards Colerne. But its history is somewhat different. Explore the artefacts on display and you will be transported to a distant world.

The pub is around 250 years old. It may originally have been built as a farmhouse, but in 1865 it was rebuilt as a beer house for local quarrymen.

Stone had been quarried at Box since early times. The tradition is that St Aldhelm identified the location of massive reserves here in the 7th century. However, the more prosaic truth is that the quarries predated St Aldhelm, having already been exploited by the Romans.

It was the building of the famous Box Tunnel – part of Brunel's Great Western Railway from London to Bath and Bristol – that greatly increased the demand for local stone. For a while, Box had one of the largest stone mines in the world. This, together with the coming of the railway, transformed the village from a farming community to an industrial area.

All the quarrymen crowding into Box needed somewhere to drink. The Quarryman's Arms must have been a rowdy place in the 19th century, a far cry from the popular bar and hotel that it has become today. So when quarrying activity began to decline in the mid-20th century, the then-owners of the Quarryman's Arms saw the need to preserve some of the pub's – and the village's – history.

They collected a range of quarrying implements and displayed them in the pub. Today the walls are covered with all sorts of tools. There are saws and picks and devices for hauling the stone blocks out of the ground, and those all-important helmets for the miners working underground. They all act as a reminder that quarrying was almost entirely a manual process and a dangerous activity. And that it was obviously thirsty work!

Walk into the small snug bar and you'll see a map of the Box stone mines. And around the pub are photographs and drawings of the quarrymen themselves. A real piece of social history.

The Quarryman's Arms is on a hill above the old stone mines. It is possible to walk up to the pub by means of a steep stepped footpath known as the 'Stairway to Heaven', passing through a nature reserve on the site of a former quarry.

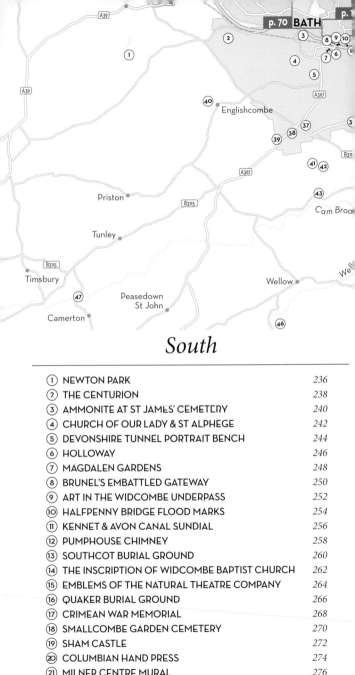

Englishcombe

Priston

Tunley

Timsbury

Wellow

Peasedown
St John

Camerton

Cam Broo

South

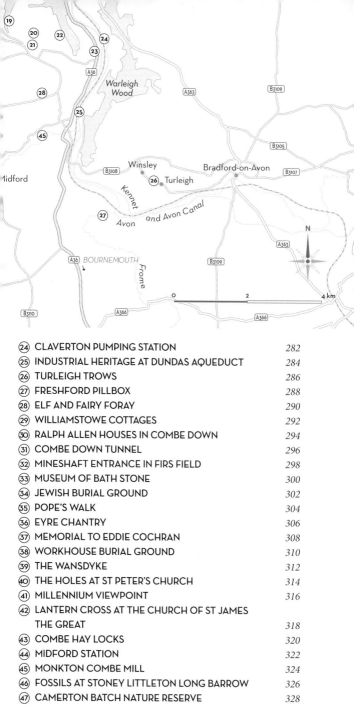

NEWTON PARK

Eighteenth-century pleasure grounds

Newton St Loe, BA2 9BN
Public access at any reasonable time
Bus U5 from St James's Parade, or drive and park in pay-and-display car park

Students at the Newton Park campus of Bath Spa University are privileged to spend their days on a Georgian country estate. The modern university buildings are clustered around a grand house once described as 'one of the finest country mansions' in 18th-century Somerset. People who are not students are unlikely to be familiar with the park and may be unaware that the public are welcome to visit and walk around the grounds.

On one side of the campus is open farmland; on the other is an unspoilt landscape garden. The pleasure grounds were laid out in 1761 by Capability Brown. They were based around two large lakes surrounded by trees; a gravel path led around the gently undulating land surrounding the lakes, with carefully created vistas along the way. Visitors can still follow the original path, passing the old ice house and an orangery designed to resemble a classical temple.

A central feature of the pleasure grounds are the remains of Newton St Loe Castle, a fortified manor house from the 14th century. The castle keep is now part of the university premises. If the door is open, you'll be able to climb the central stairway, but unfortunately you can't peek

inside the rooms! Beyond the keep is the 15th-century gatehouse, leading to a small garden and the old stables.

The whole estate now belongs to the Duchy of Cornwall. After you've walked around the lake and the castle remains, there is plenty more to explore. You can see a walled garden (formerly a kitchen garden) on the other side of the campus, and a pleasant walk through farmland takes you to the village of Newton St Loe, where you'll find a farm shop and cafe.

Ammonites in Newton St Loe

You may notice several large ammonites built into walls and buildings in Newton Park and the neighbouring village. These are a reminder that the area is known for the richness of its fossils, which led to Newton St Loe being declared a geological Site of Special Scientific Interest in 1992.

THE CENTURION

A Grade II listed 1960s pub with a Roman theme

Poolemead Road, Twerton, BA2 1QR
centurion-inn.edan.io
Bus 5 from Avon Street to Walwyn Close

The Centurion is a curiosity. A Grade II listed 1960s pub, preserved for its uncompromising modernity … and a pub with a Roman theme, a homage to the distant past.

When the Centurion was listed as a heritage building in 2018, it was described as a 'historic post-war pub'. It was built at a time when thousands of new pubs were being constructed on modern housing estates, partly due to new demand and partly to replace those damaged by wartime bombing.

So why was the Centurion singled out for preservation? One reason was that its architecture typifies 1960s design. New pubs catered for their communities, with large car parks and light, spacious interiors intended to suggest modern, comfortable social spaces.

The Centurion did all of this and more. In keeping with the times, it was designed to fit in with its surroundings while making a bold visual statement. So it is fashioned from a variety of building materials, including reconstituted Bath stone, glass, concrete and steel. And while the front is striking and modern, the sides and back are lower and more modest, blending in with the surrounding houses.

The building is a rectangular block on four floors, with large windows and sharp angles. A particular feature is that it is built onto a steep hillside: the design takes full advantage both of the slope and of the views.

Although changes have inevitably been made, the Centurion is substantially unaltered, retaining its original exterior and much of the interior layout. And it is still very much a local, with skittles, darts and screens for watching sport.

There is another reason why the Centurion was chosen as an exemplar of post-war pub architecture. Many of these pubs were themed. And the Centurion chose quite a striking theme: the building may be modern but its name and decorative features pay tribute to the city's Roman heritage.

You might have to look carefully to find the fragment of Roman mosaic flooring hanging on a dark wall near the entrance. But you will have no problem spotting the large bronze centurion, complete with armour, helmet and shield, who stands above the upper floors of the pub and greets you as you arrive.

AMMONITE AT
ST JAMES' CEMETERY

An unusual headstone

87 Lower Bristol Road, BA2 3BQ
Daily, 8.30am–7.30pm

Bath's many cemeteries are full of elaborate or eccentric tombstones. But perhaps one of the most unusual is the large ammonite headstone in St James' Cemetery on the Lower Bristol Road.

You will find the grave on the far left of the graveyard. And when you look closely, you'll see that it's not just a single fossil. Apart from the main stone (which is more than half a metre high), a series of smaller ammonites line each side of the grave. They are all estimated to be around 66 million years old.

This is the burial place of John Williams, who died on 12 April 1907 at the age of 68. He was an engine driver who moved to Bath to work on the Somerset & Dorset Joint Railway. Little more is known about him other than that he lived with his family at Sydenham Buildings, very close to the cemetery. However, he must have been one of the very first drivers on the Somerset & Dorset, which only opened in 1875.

So why the ammonites? Time and weathering have made it hard to read the inscription but, according to a 1932 report in the *Bath Chronicle*, the gravestone states that Williams was 'a keen geologist and ardent lover of Nature'. So perhaps his family, or a fellow amateur geologist, felt this to be a fitting memorial.

Another question arises: where did the ammonites come from? Although the area is rich in fossils, you might have expected such a large specimen to have attracted some attention. But no record seems to have survived and it remains a mystery.

Gothic Revival chapels

While you're in the cemetery, have a look at the rather fine pair of Gothic Revival chapels at the centre, built in the 1860s. Unusually, St James' Cemetery, which dates from 1861, was open to both Anglicans and Nonconformists. This meant that two separate chapels were required, one for each group. The chapels are now sadly neglected and you can't go inside but you can admire the arches, buttresses and other architectural features from the outside.

CHURCH OF
OUR LADY & ST ALPHEGE

Modern church, ancient design

Oldfield Lane, BA2 3NR
saintalphege.org.uk
See website for service times; also open on Heritage Open Days
Bus 1 from Avon Street to Moorland Road

Among the suburban dwellings of Oldfield Park is an early Christian basilica … or so it might seem at first sight. But look closer and you'll see that the Church of Our Lady & St Alphege is not ancient but modern, a masterpiece of 20th-century design.

This was the third Roman Catholic church in Bath (the others being St John the Evangelist on North Parade and St Mary's on Julian Road). The architect commissioned to build it was the renowned Sir Giles Gilbert Scott, who was also responsible for Liverpool's Anglican Cathedral and for the classic red telephone box (see p. 136).

Scott took as his inspiration Santa Maria in Cosmedin, a 6th-century church in Rome. It was not a straightforward replica, but a reinterpretation using modern building materials. Scott himself regarded it as one of his finest works. The church was completed in 1929 but not consecrated until 1954, a thousand years after the birth of St Alphege.

As you approach the church, note the Italianate exterior with arches and columns – all built from local Bath stone, apart from the roof tiles which were imported from Lombardy. The interior is magnificent, simple in design but intricate in detail. The lights are tiny starbursts, and the floor a mosaic of coloured linoleum.

Pay particular attention to the carvings. Around the walls are the Stations of the Cross, and other figurative designs on the capitals at the top of each pillar tell the story of the church and the people associated with it. There are scenes from the lives of St Alphege and the Virgin Mary, and images of those who designed and built the church.

The church is open for services on Sundays and during the week, and there are occasional Open Days. Although there are no regular visiting times, you may sometimes find it open as you pass by.

St Alphege was a Bath saint, born in Weston in 954. He was known for his asceticism and eventually became Archbishop of Canterbury. He was captured by Viking raiders in Canterbury and martyred by them when he refused to be ransomed. There is a chapel dedicated to St Alphege in Bath Abbey.

DEVONSHIRE TUNNEL PORTRAIT BENCH

Honouring local heroes

At the western entrance to the Devonshire Tunnel: access via Bloomfield Green, BA2 2AB
Bus 4a from St James's Parade to Bear Flat

Walkers and cyclists emerging from the Devonshire Tunnel (a former railway tunnel on the Two Tunnels Greenway path) close to Bloomfield Green will see some ghostly figures in the grass on the left. These are part of a 'portrait bench' created by Sustrans to honour local heroes.

Sustrans maintain cycle and hiking routes across the country. A number of artworks have been created along their routes. Many of these are sculptures but there are several portrait benches, all with local significance. The people to be honoured on the Devonshire Tunnel portrait bench were chosen by children from the nearby Oldfield Park Junior School.

Three life-sized outline steel figures now stand beside the path. The first is a Roman centurion: not an individual but a representative of an era. He commemorates 300 years of Roman rule in Bath, and the creation of the spa on which the city's later wealth was founded.

The second figure is that of Harry Patch, the 'last fighting Tommy' (see below). And, finally, there is Amy Williams, a former skeleton racer from Bath who won a gold medal at the 2010 Winter Olympics. Williams herself unveiled the portrait bench when it was installed in 2013.

Today the bench is a place for passers-by to stop and rest in the company of people who made a difference to the city.

Harry Patch, the 'last fighting Tommy'

Harry Patch, who died in 2009 at the age of 111, was the last surviving soldier of any nationality to have fought in the trenches during the First World War. At the time of his death, he was also the oldest man in Europe and the last British male to have been born in the 19th century. In later life, he became known for his views on the horror and futility of war.

Patch was born in Combe Down and lived in Bath for much of his life. A plaque marks the house at 5 Gladstone Place where he lived after the war. You can see his grave at St Michael's Church in Monkton Combe.

HOLLOWAY

A historic route into the city

Holloway, BA2 4PX

If you leave Bear Flat along the quiet road known as Holloway, you will be following a route into Bath that has been trodden for centuries. You'll also walk along a historic raised pavement and pass some of the oldest buildings in the city.

It was once thought that Holloway was part of the Fosse Way, the Roman road that passed through Bath on the way from Lincoln to Exeter. However, although long stretches of the Fosse Way remain elsewhere, the route through Bath is unclear.

What is not in doubt is that this was a very busy road in the Middle Ages. It was the main road out of town to the south and would have been lined with houses, including the grand residences of the city's wool merchants.

'Holloway' (a corruption of 'hollow way') is a name used for medieval roads around the country – roads with heavy traffic would gradually sink below the level of the surrounding land. This effect is likely to have been exacerbated in Bath when wagons carrying stone from the local quarries made their way south from the city.

There is an alternative explanation for the name. Perhaps it means 'holy way', a reference to the fact that pilgrims once walked along the road on their way to Glastonbury. It is further suggested that the horse trough beside the road (see below) was in fact a holy well from which pilgrims would stop to drink.

Holloway declined in importance in the 1770s after the Wells Road was built. But you can still see the hollowed-out road at the bottom of Beechen Cliff, winding downhill from Bear Flat. The long section of raised pavement, with flagstones and iron railings, was built around 1810. The road passes several very old buildings, including the historic Magdalen Chapel.

The hills around the city were noted for their natural springs, which supplied fresh water for the local population. The horse trough by the side of Holloway would have been used to refresh passing pack animals and possibly thirsty drivers as well. The current rather ornate structure was built in the mid-19th century and features a moralistic poem with the opening line, 'A man of kindness to his beast is kind'.

MAGDALEN GARDENS

A lesser-known park on Beechen Cliff

Holloway, BA2 4PX
Bus 4 from St James's Parade to St Mary's Buildings

For many people Beechen Cliff is synonymous with Alexandra Park, the hilltop space with its famous Lookout and spectacular views across the city. But on the hillside between Alexandra Park and Holloway is another – smaller and much lesser known – park, Magdalen Gardens.

Beechen Cliff was always known as a place to walk and admire the views. Jane Austen spoke of visiting the area and featured it in her novel *Northanger Abbey*. But it became especially popular after the railway came to Bath. Visitors would leave the train and walk up the hill for their first view of the city, passing through Magdalen Gardens on the way.

The gardens were laid out as a pleasure ground in 1902, with lawns and flowerbeds. The area was subsequently neglected and the park fell into ruin. In recent years the council has worked with local volunteers to restore Magdalen Gardens. Overgrown shrubs and trees were cleared, paths were laid, and native bulbs and flowers were planted.

If you visit the gardens today, you'll find a small, quiet park on a steep slope. Paths wind their way up the hill and you can stop to read the information boards or enjoy the vista ahead of you. It might not be quite the same view as from Alexandra Park, but it is still impressive looking down to the Chapel of St Mary Magdalen towards the city.

Beside the park is Beechen Cliff woodland. Much of this area was once covered by small cottages, which were mostly destroyed by wartime bombing. Today the woodland is managed, and paths between the trees allow you to continue your walk from Magdalen Gardens uphill to Alexandra Park.

Jacob's Ladder

An alternative way of climbing up Beechen Cliff to the Alexandra Park Lookout is by walking up Jacob's Ladder, a stepped footpath created around 1915. Starting at Calton Road, a long series of steps takes you right to the top of the hill. But don't attempt this unless you're reasonably fit – there are lots of steps and they're steep and uneven.

BRUNEL'S EMBATTLED GATEWAY

A showpiece of railway architecture

Churchill Bridge roundabout, BA2 4PZ

The building of the Great Western Railway in Bath in the early 1840s caused all sorts of structural dilemmas. Fortunately the engineer in charge of the project was Isambard Kingdom Brunel, who combined a genius for solving practical problems with a keen interest in aesthetic design. One of the most prominent features of his railway as it runs through Bath is the embattled gateway to the west of Skew Bridge.

The problems to be overcome might have defeated a lesser man. First there was the city's topography, with its steep hills and the winding River Avon with its propensity to flooding. Then there was the insistence of the city fathers that the railway should be accessible to Bath's citizens but should not run through the Georgian city itself.

Brunel's solution was a series of bridges and viaducts, and a railway station perched upon 20 arches. Where the railway required the demolition of workers' homes in Twerton, the occupants were offered new (and apparently rather uncomfortable) houses built into the archways, perhaps the only example of domestic architecture by Brunel.

The new railway employed a variety of architectural styles. There were graceful cast iron bridges where the line cut through Sydney Gardens, and Jacobean-style bridges and viaducts at Twerton. And a medieval Gothic section was built to the west of the station.

The castellated viaduct that stands opposite the end of Southgate is designed in the manner of a Tudor castle. It has a pair of semi-octagonal towers, a battlemented top, archways and arrow slits. The central door originally led to two rooms. One was used as a police station; the other was a mortuary for when bodies were pulled out of the river.

We are not entirely sure why Brunel chose such an extravagant design for this section of the viaduct. It may have been intended to suggest a grand entrance to the city, a reminder of the old South Gate, which was demolished in 1755. Or it might have been an echo of Brunel's grand Gothic railway station at Temple Meads in Bristol.

It is also possible that the gateway was designed simply as a statement, to be seen by the citizens of Bath as they walked south from the city, and to demonstrate the importance of the railway. If this was the case, there seems to have been no corresponding desire to impress the inhabitants of Widcombe: walk to the back of the gateway and you'll see that the other side is extremely plain!

ART IN THE WIDCOMBE UNDERPASS

⑨

A subterranean mural

Claverton Street, close to Churchill Bridge roundabout, BA2 4JP

Bath is a World Heritage Site, so – unlike many other cities – it doesn't have much if anything in the way of murals or street art. An exception is the colourful mural in the Widcombe underpass, although the drivers who thunder overhead on the busy A36 are unlikely to be aware of its existence.

Historically, Widcombe was separated from the old town of Bath by the River Avon. Since 1869 it has been possible to cross the river on foot via the Halfpenny Bridge, but in recent times a second barrier has emerged: the stream of traffic on Claverton Street, now the A36.

An underpass was built in the 1960s to allow pedestrians to cross the road safely, to access the railway station and the city centre. However, the passage was subject to flooding and over time it became filled with rubbish and unpleasant to use. Local residents started to avoid the subway, particularly after dark, and a campaign was launched for its renovation.

After a period of closure and refurbishment, the underpass was reopened in 2019 with improved lighting, CCTV and floodproofing. But it was still visually unattractive. The final improvement came in 2021 with the creation of a mural covering both sides of the passage and the ramps at either end.

The new mural was painted by Dan Wilson and Tom Webb, using designs created by Sarah Ovens, a local artist. Its theme was 'Welcome to Widcombe, where Bath City meets the countryside'. As well as brightening the place up and discouraging graffiti, it was intended to highlight the local area.

Now as you walk through the tunnel, you are greeted by pictures of local landmarks such as Priory Park Landscape Garden and the Kennet & Avon Canal, interspersed with images of grass and trees, flowers and animals.

Widcombe underpass might once have been a place to avoid, or at least to get through as quickly as possible. But now it is bright and cheery, an invitation to stop and enjoy the artwork.

HALFPENNY BRIDGE
FLOOD MARKS

Recording natural disasters

Footpath beneath the south side of the Halfpenny Bridge, BA1 1SX

Many of Bath's river and canal bridges have interesting bits of graffiti and builders' marks etched into the stone beneath them. But you'll find a different sort of mark underneath the Halfpenny Bridge – a series of flood marks dating back to 1866.

Follow the footpath that goes beneath the bridge on the Widcombe side of the Avon and you'll see 14 dates carved into the stone, covering a period of around 100 years. Look down to the water below you, then up to the highest mark. On 15 November 1894 the river rose to around 6 metres above its normal height: the prospect of such a volume of water advancing on people's homes must have been terrifying.

The latest recorded date is 5 December 1960. This is not because people lost interest in recording water levels but because flood prevention measures – most notably the redesign of Pulteney Weir in 1968 – have meant that serious flooding is now thankfully a thing of the past. So you can stop and look at the Halfpenny Bridge flood marks without any fear of the water lapping around your feet.

Flood marks have been used throughout history to note the height to which water has risen during an extreme weather event. They may at one time have been marked as a historic record, a piece of community folklore. Or they may simply have been a sign of relief and gratitude for having survived a natural disaster. However, more recently they have been a valuable source of information for scientists, researchers and those involved in flood prevention.

Bath was very prone to flooding. The Romans knew this and raised the level of some of their buildings to protect them from the water. The Georgian builders of Bath went further: all the new houses and buildings in the Lower Town were constructed on raised foundations.

However, this did not stop the water from rising. The less fortunate people dwelling on the other side of the river had to live with the very real possibility of their houses and gardens being submerged.

KENNET & AVON CANAL SUNDIAL

Where local time still prevails

Kennet & Avon Canal, south of Horseshoe Walk road bridge, BA2 6DG

As you walk along the Kennet & Avon Canal from the River Avon towards Sydney Gardens, you'll spot a large sundial beside the

towpath. But don't expect to set your watch by it: this sundial has a slightly idiosyncratic relationship with time.

Around the plinth are carved the words, 'Time is the waterway of all our days; We are dreamers on its banks.' The sundial was commissioned in 2010 to commemorate the 200th anniversary of the opening of the Kennet & Avon Canal; it was designed to mark the passage of time while also alluding to the industrial past.

It marks time as it would have been when the canal opened in 1810, when time was measured very differently from now. Going back to the earliest human history, time was measured according to the sun, with midday occurring when the sun was immediately overhead. This would vary as you moved from east to west.

In an era before mass communication, it didn't really matter that local time was slightly different wherever you went. It was only with the creation of the railways – and strict railway timetables – that it became necessary to have the same time zone across the country. In 1840 the Great Western Railway introduced 'Railway Time', standardising times along its network. And in 1880 Greenwich Mean Time (GMT) was adopted across the UK.

The Kennet & Avon sundial is set to 'Widcombe Time', which was in use on this stretch of canal back in 1810. This would have been approximately 11 minutes later than GMT, a fact that was of little significance in the early industrial age.

The sundial was intended to highlight the city's industrial history alongside its better-known Georgian heritage. The gnomon (the part of the sundial that casts a shadow) is in the form of a stylised bargepole, and around the dial plate is a map of the canal, together with markings showing the time of day.

On one side of the gnomon is a long list of goods that were transported along the canal in the 19th century: local limestone and Fuller's earth as well as porter, eggs, tallow and many other commodities. On the other side is a list of those who used and worked on the canal. Alongside navvies, bargemasters and lock keepers you will also find 'gongoozlers' (people who liked to stand and watch the activity along the canal).

PUMPHOUSE CHIMNEY

*The improbably ornate Victorian chimney
of a former pumping station*

Kennet & Avon Canal, Bathwick, BA2 4JF

Walk along the Kennet & Avon Canal past Sydney Gardens and towards the railway station and you'll come to a tall Victorian structure of shaped and carved Bath stone. At first, you might think that it's some sort of memorial but in fact it's an industrial building: a chimney for a long-disappeared pumping station.

When the canal was constructed at the end of the 18th century, the engineers created a series of locks to cope with the fact that Bath is surrounded by hills. The pumping station was built around 1830 as part of a system for moving water to the locks higher up the canal. It was powered by a boiler, and a chimney was needed to carry away steam and waste materials.

So far, so good. But look closely at the chimney and you'll see that it seems rather too grand for its purpose. Built of blocks of stone and iron bands, it has a plinth and carved scrolls and is topped by a very ornate pot.

There seem to be two reasons for this unexpected splendour. The owners of the canal were proud of their undertaking and wanted the waterway and its associated buildings to complement the city's Georgian architecture. At the same time, they wanted to forestall any possible complaints from local residents about ugly industrial structures.

Despite the solid Victorian workmanship, the chimney was close to collapse by the end of the 20th century. But it has now been restored to its former glory, the restorers making sure to preserve the very slight (two-degree) lean that had developed since the chimney was first built.

The pumphouse chimney is once more a feature of canal-side walks. And on sunny days you may be able to sit on a bench and grab a coffee from the pop-up cafe in the nearby Pump Shed.

SOUTHCOT BURIAL GROUND

A hidden oasis in the heart of the city

Bottom of Lyncombe Hill, Widcombe, BA2 4PF
01225 338727
admin@bptrust.org.uk
Open on Heritage Open Days and at other times by appointment

One of Bath's lesser-known cemeteries is the old Baptist burial ground at the bottom of Lyncombe Hill. Home to hundreds of unmarked graves and identified by an unusual system of row markers, it is now preserved both for its social history and as a nature haven.

The burial ground can be seen through the gates on Lyncombe Hill at any time. It is only open to the public on Heritage Open Days (and occasionally at other times). It can also be visited by appointment – phone or email for information.

Like other Nonconformist religious groups, the Baptist church needed a place to bury its dead. In 1810 a part of the grounds of Southcot House was granted to the church by one of its deacons, Opie Smith, a local brewer and land developer.

It is thought that more than 1,000 people were buried here. According to the register, 324 of these were children, many of them under the age of 2. But there are few tombstones as most of the congregation were from poor working-class families and could not afford to pay for memorials.

Most people were buried in unmarked graves. However, relatives of the deceased could locate their burial place through a system of carved row markers in the ground and on the wall. A typical grave position might be described as 'In the letter D 5 feet 6 inches from the lower wall'.

The last burial at Southcot took place in 1907 and the records of those buried there were subsequently lost. The ground might have become completely overgrown and forgotten – or developed for housing – if the cemetery had not been acquired by the Bath Preservation Trust in the 1990s.

Today the Southcot Burial Ground is maintained as a garden and wildlife oasis. You can still see the remains of the grave markers in the wall and in the ground. But bulbs have been planted, there are nesting boxes in the trees and beekeepers have hives here.

A tree trail through the cemetery features a variety of both native and exotic species. Some of these have religious significance – look out for the Judas tree, the cedar and the so-called 'tree of Heaven'.

THE INSCRIPTION OF WIDCOMBE BAPTIST CHURCH

The thorn and the fir tree

Pultney Road, BA2 4JR
widcombebaptist.org

Widcombe Baptist Church occupies a large and eclectic building overlooking the Kennet & Avon Canal. On one side, on the old Sunday School building, it bears what seems a rather cryptic message, which reads, 'Instead of the thorn shall come up the fir tree, and it shall be to the Lord for a name.'

To understand this inscription you need to know that the schoolroom was built on the site of the Canal Tavern. This tavern had been in existence since at least 1837 and it was probably built to serve the growing population of canal- and railway-workers in Dolemeads.

In some ways the Canal Tavern seems to have been well appointed. It had its own brewery and lots of facilities for customers, including skittles, crib boards and a bagatelle table. However, the atmosphere must have been less than salubrious as we are told that there were several spittoons, and an open urinal in the skittle alley.

The tavern building was adjacent to the Baptist Church, at that time known as the Ebenezer Chapel. The presumably rowdy behaviour of the tavern's customers must have exasperated the congregation. Furthermore, many of the churchgoers belonged to the growing temperance movement and resented the very existence of a nearby pub. So you can see why it might have been regarded as a 'thorn' in the side of the church and of the local authorities.

It must have seemed like a miracle when the church was able to buy the pub building at the time that it was looking for premises for a schoolroom. In 1910 the foundation stone was laid for the new Sunday School building, and an inscription was carved above the door.

The 'fir tree' that replaced the thorn was the schoolroom itself. This seems to be an Old Testament reference: if the Canal Tavern represented the 'unnatural evil' of drink, then the fir tree was a symbol of nature, truth and goodness.

An additional curiosity of the Baptist Church is the religious texts placed prominently on the pyramid-shaped roof. These include the words 'Prepare to meet your God' and 'Christ died for our sins'. They are visible from several places and can be seen by visitors approaching Bath by train. Painted around 1903, they caused some controversy in the past but are now accepted as part of the urban landscape.

EMBLEMS OF THE NATURAL THEATRE COMPANY

Spot the stone faces

Widcombe Institute, Widcombe Hill, BA2 6AA

If you walk up Widcombe Hill and stop to look at the Old Church Room, you'll see some curious stone faces staring down at you. These are the emblems of the Natural Theatre Company, which made its home here in 1997.

Founded in 1970, the Natural Theatre Company is a community organisation that has established itself as a leading practitioner of street theatre, performing in the city and around the country. Over the years, the company has created a range of bespoke and sometimes quirky characters. Some are comic and some are historical: you may have met some of their costumed Roman citizens who chat to visitors at the Roman Baths Museum.

Although the Natural Theatre continues its off-stage theatrical work, it now has a permanent home on Widcombe Hill. The building itself is interesting, having been constructed in 1882 as the Church Room and Institute. It was planned and used as a Sunday school, but apparently also incorporated a billiard room and boxing arena.

The theatre company converted the interior of the building but they naturally wanted to put their own stamp on the outside. So they commissioned a group of four stone sculptures to support a new steel canopy. (The canopy was intended to be covered by a glass roof but the money ran out …)

Carved by masonry students from Bath College in 1995, the sculptures represent some of the company's best-known characters. Three of them are heads only: Nanny Face (with glasses and a stern expression), Georgian (with curly hair and a carnival mask) and Conehead. (Incidentally Conehead – or Egg-head as he is sometimes known – can also be seen on the other side of Bath, on the Wall of Walcot, see p. 114).

The fourth sculpture is a full-sized figure and the unofficial emblem of the Natural Theatre Company. This is Flowerpot Man, formally dressed but with a flowerpot in place of a head. His hands and jacket were modelled on a photograph of Prince Charles (as he was then).

QUAKER BURIAL GROUND

A secret garden in Widcombe

Clarendon Road, BA2 4NJ
07818 760042
bathquakers.org/quaker-burial-ground-widcombe
Occasional open days or phone for gate code
Bus 2 from Dorchester Street to Bewdley Road

Behind a wooden gate in Clarendon Road is an old Quaker burial ground. But no one is buried here any more. The space has become a quiet walled garden, accessible only to those who know the code.

Prior to 1880, people who had not been baptised were generally refused burial in Church of England cemeteries. This meant that Nonconformist groups had to provide their own graveyards. The first Quaker burial place in Bath was in Bathford, but in 1827 a more central plot of land in Widcombe was acquired from the estate of a local Quaker.

More than 200 people were buried here, the last interment taking place in 1974. Although burials have now stopped, Quakers may still have their ashes scattered in the garden.

For a while the land fell into disuse and became overgrown. But eventually it was decided to create a garden as a space for quiet reflection. The gravestones were removed and replaced around the perimeter wall. Then the garden was planted with trees and flowers, and paths were mown through the long grass.

Walking into the burial ground today you are likely to be struck by the lack of ostentation in the graves. In keeping with the Quaker tradition of plainness, there are no ornate tombs: stones were recorded simply with name, age and date of death, and no further information. Indeed, prior to 1850 no stones were permitted at all.

The 'Cremation Wall' at the back of the garden lists the names of those whose ashes were scattered prior to 2007. However, no memorials have been recorded since that date.

The burial ground is a secluded place, with seats and a small covered area for use in the event of rain. It has trees, wild flowers and garden flowers in the borders. In the summer you'll see lots of white poppies, a symbol of the Quaker commitment to peace.

The garden is now sometimes used for Quaker meetings and gatherings and there are occasional public open days. But anyone may visit and enjoy the peace and quiet: just phone and request the code for the gate.

CRIMEAN WAR MEMORIAL

A war memorial with unusual features

Bath Abbey Cemetery, Perrymead, BA2 5AJ
Bus 2 from Dorchester Street to Perrymead

War memorials only really became widespread after the First World War. However, earlier monuments do exist, like Sir Bevil Grenville's monument on Lansdown Hill (see p. 146). Another example is the Crimean War memorial at the top of the carriage drive in Bath Abbey Cemetery. And this one has a few curious features of its own.

Many Bath men fought in the Crimean War. The very first casualty of the campaign was a local man: William Shell, an ordinary seaman whose widowed mother lived in Hampton Row. His name is recorded on the obelisk, as are those of John Bythesea and William Johnstone, who were the second and third recipients of the newly created Victoria Cross for bravery.

In all, the memorial lists eleven men from Bath who gave their lives in the war. It is unusual in giving the names of both officers and other ranks: most monuments of the time only recognised those of the officer class.

Another peculiarity is that this is a local memorial, remembering the fallen men of Bath rather than those of a particular regiment. In 1855 a public subscription was raised for the benefit of wounded soldiers passing through the city. Part of the surplus from the subscription was used to fund the building of the memorial stone the following year.

As well as the names of those who died, the 6-metre-high stone obelisk shows the names of various Crimean War battles, including Balaklava and Sevastopol. There are moulded laurel leaves and a quotation from Ecclesiastes: 'There is a time to die.'

Bath Abbey Cemetery was opened in 1844 when the Abbey itself had no further space for burials. As with many Victorian cemeteries it had a dual purpose, being designed as a healthy outdoor space as well as a graveyard. It was built on a hill to give commanding views across the city and laid out with trees and pathways between the graves. The cemetery closed in 1995 but it is still a green space to be enjoyed by local citizens. It has started to return to nature and hosts a wide variety of plant and animal life.

SMALLCOMBE GARDEN CEMETERY

Following a social history trail between the graves

Smallcombe Vale, BA2 6DD
Can be visited at any time
smallcombegardencemetery.org
Bus 20 from Grand Parade to The Tyning, then 13-min. walk

Smallcombe Garden Cemetery is hidden away in a small valley to the south-east of Bath. It is now closed to new plots but maintained as a nature area. It is also a place where you can discover a bit of local heritage by following a social history trail between the graves.

The cemetery is in two sections, with the smaller part for Nonconformist burials. It opened in 1856, when St Mary's in Bathwick was full, and it remained in use until 1988. It subsequently began to deteriorate but has now been restored as an oasis for peaceful walks and a place to discover the stories behind the names on the graves.

When the cemetery opened, the cost of burials was kept low. This meant that people from all walks of life, from artisans to the aristocracy, could be buried here. As you might expect of a cemetery from the mid-Victorian era, it has lots of very ornate and decorative headstones. There are around 70,000 graves in total. The Social History Trail highlights just 13 of these, the aim being to give 'an insight into life in Victorian and Edwardian Bath'. Each grave in the trail is marked with a QR code that leads you to a wealth of online information about the individual (or group of individuals in the case of a family grave).

Those featured in the trail were involved in commerce, the arts and the armed forces. There are well-known local families, such as the Milsoms who gave their name to Bath's famous shopping street. And others who were once well known, like the Clack family, butchers and fishmongers of Slippery Lane (see p. 100).

Fred Weatherly was a barrister but better known for the songs he wrote (including 'Danny Boy' and 'Roses of Picardy'). And Moses Pickwick (landlord of a coaching inn) had his name immortalised in one of Charles Dickens' most famous books.

Some of these memorials are very elaborate. The family tomb of John Hay Maitland Hardyman, a poet and hero of the First World War, has a marble statue of a child with a bunch of flowers. And Mildred Farrar and Mary Loder (artists who were both descended from King Charles II and Nell Gwynn) have an intricately carved stone bench. It has angel sculptures at either end and an artist's palette etched into the back of the seat.

SHAM CASTLE

Not medieval, not a real castle either: a Gothic folly on Claverton Down

Golf Course Road, BA2 6JG
Nearest bus stop: Quarry Road
Sham Castle is on Claverton Down, close to Bath Golf Club (a local eccentricity is to call hills 'downs')

Walking through the centre of Bath, you may occasionally catch a glimpse of a castle high up on the hillside. Perhaps a medieval fortress, you might think, as the yellow stone towers gleam in the sunlight.

It's the colour of the stone that gives away Sham Castle's real age. It was built for the entrepreneur Ralph Allen in 1762, using recently dug stone from his quarries. Not only is it not medieval; it's not a real castle either. It's a classic 18th-century folly, just a facade with nothing behind it.

The Gothic-style folly consists of two semicircular towers flanking an archway, with square towers at the sides. It comes complete with battlements and arrow-slits. However, walk around the back and the building is much plainer; it was obviously intended only to be viewed from the front. But you do get a nice view of the city through the archway …

It is generally assumed that Ralph Allen had the castle built so that he could view it from his town house (see p. 44) in the centre of Bath (it would still be visible from there today if a large tree hadn't grown up in the way). However, there are alternative explanations. He may have wanted to create employment for local stonemasons (Allen was known as a philanthropist) or just to show off his local stone.

A bench in front of the castle – ideal for admiring the view – carries a quote from Jane Austen's novel *Northanger Abbey* in which Catherine Morland says, 'I really believe I shall always be talking of Bath when I am home again – I do love it so very much.' Austen would certainly have been familiar with Sham Castle: perhaps it inspired her Gothic-obsessed heroine?

COLUMBIAN HAND PRESS

*A Victorian printing press once used
by Sir Isaac Pitman*

University of Bath Library, Claverton Down, Bath BA2 7AY
library.bath.ac.uk
Open 24 hours
U1 Unibus from Bath Abbey to Arrivals Square

In the foyer of Bath University Library is a large and ornate piece of Victorian machinery: this is a Columbian hand press that once belonged to the Pitman Press, a printing firm owned by Sir Isaac Pitman.

Pitman, who lived most of his life in Bath, is probably best known for his invention of a method of shorthand writing. He was also a teacher who wanted to reform the spelling of the English language. In both cases his motive was the saving of time, his motto being 'Time saved is life gained.'

Together with his sons, Pitman set up a publishing company which printed his works on spelling reform and other educational materials. (His other achievements included the creation of the very first correspondence course – on the shorthand system – and being Vice President of the Vegetarian Society.)

The University Library has a vast archive of material relating to Pitman, with thousands of books, journals and other items concerning the invention of shorthand, the work of the Pitman Press and the varied interests of Pitman and his family.

In pride of place – and on public display – is the printing press that catches your eye as soon as you walk through the door. This was given to the university in 2007 by the Bath Press (successor to the Pitman Press). Manufactured in 1839, it is an example of a Columbian printing press, an American design that was very popular with 19th-century publishers. Columbian presses were heavy, hand-operated machines but had the advantage of being able to print large items such as newspapers very quickly. They were also known for being very ornate, with elaborate symbolism.

The Pitman machine is typical of early Columbian presses. Look for the characteristic eagle (symbol of the United States), the fruit and flowers, and the strange serpentine creatures. The latter are apparently intended to be dolphins, symbols of wisdom and learning.

If you're in the centre of Bath, stop to look at the Kingston Buildings, from where Pitman once ran his business. You'll see the name carved into the stone using Pitman's phonetic alphabet – KIᴎSTON BILDIᴎZ.

MILNER CENTRE MURAL

Evolutionary features in a modern building

Milner Centre for Evolution, Bath University, Claverton Down, BA2 7AZ
bath.ac.uk/research-centres/milner-centre-for-evolution
U1 Unibus from Bath Abbey to North Road

The University of Bath campus is known for its pioneering modern architecture. One of the most striking buildings is the Milner Centre for Evolution, with what appears to be an abstract mural on one wall. But look closer and you'll see that there is more to the design than first meets the eye.

Opened in 2018, the Milner Centre is a cross-disciplinary research facility that addresses 'fundamental questions about evolution'. The new purpose-built structure incorporates the latest thinking in functional design. It was apparently influenced by the Pixar Studios in California, encouraging flexibility, social interaction and collaborative working.

Staff and students from the university worked closely with the architectural team. It was important that the building had design features that reflected its purpose and surroundings. For instance, as well as being a stunning modern building, it was constructed from local Bath stone and included tall windows as a homage to the city's Georgian architecture.

The concept of evolution is woven into the fabric of the building. Inside there is a coffee table made from fossils and a nautilus-inspired spiral on the ceiling (which can be glimpsed from the outside).

But for the casual visitor the main item of interest is the Alignment Wall. As you approach, it looks like a piece of abstract art in varying shades of blue. However, there is nothing abstract about it. It is a carefully designed series of colour-coded gene sequences that chart the evolutionary path from fish to humans. Created, perhaps, to emphasise the patterns inherent in nature.

Many of the university buildings were built in the so-called brutalist style by the influential architects Alison and Peter Smithson. These include the Second Arts Building, designed around the movement of the sun to maximise the use of natural light. Look out too for the steel, glass and concrete Amenity Building and for the Schools of Architecture & Building Engineering, featuring a spectacularly idiosyncratic use of varying spaces, sizes and angles.

BUSHEY NORWOOD
STANDING STONES

An unsolved mystery

Claverton Down, BA2 7JX
Bus 20 from Grand Parade to Sports Training Village (stop D)

Bushey Norwood is a large parkland area on Claverton Down, close to Bath University. It is mostly a place for ramblers, but keen-eyed walkers will spot a number of standing stones whose origin and purpose remain a mystery.

The area around Bushey Norwood is owned by the National Trust and it forms part of the Skyline Trail, a circular walk around the hills overlooking the city. It is a pleasant expanse of trees and meadowland, but move away from the path and you'll see lots of large stones. Most of them are close to the ground, on their own or in groups. But there are three standing stones, one with curious holes in it.

There are all sorts of theories about the stones and how they got there. Previous quarrying activity in the area has obviously disturbed the landscape but this would not account for the stones that have been dug out of the ground and set upright.

A popular explanation is that they are the remains of a prehistoric stone circle or avenue. However, there is no mention of it in the meticulous accounts of the 18th-century antiquarians who catalogued the country's ancient monuments. So if it is indeed a neolithic site, most of it must have disappeared some centuries ago.

Others say that the stones were marker posts for a racecourse. This theory seems less plausible as the stones don't really look like race markers. And although it is thought that there was once a racecourse on Claverton Down, its location is uncertain.

Other stories abound. Perhaps one stone marks the site of a duel in 1788. Or one was erected by Henry Duncan Skrine in memory of a favourite racehorse. The latter theory is interesting in that Skrine was not born until 1815 and the stones were first mentioned in writing in the 1820s. So perhaps they were placed at different times and there is a different explanation for each one.

And what about those curious holes? Surprisingly, we don't even know whether they are the result of weathering or of human activity. They are just another mystery!

RALPH ALLEN'S MAUSOLEUM

Stately resting place of a Bath grandee

St Mary the Virgin churchyard, Claverton, BA2 7BG
Bus D1 from Guildhall to village, then 6-min. walk

The tiny village of Claverton sits in the shadow of the American Museum and Gardens. Few visitors venture into the village itself or to the churchyard of St Mary the Virgin. Those who do will be rewarded by the sight of a large mausoleum, the final resting place of Ralph Allen.

Ralph Allen (1693–1764) is one of the most important figures in the history of Bath. He made his fortune twice over: once by his reforms to the English postal system and again by quarrying the famous yellow Bath stone that became synonymous with the city's architecture. An influential local figure and notable philanthropist, he was friendly with famous artists and writers of the time and is said to have been the model for Squire Allworthy in Henry Fielding's novel Tom Jones.

So it seems appropriate that he should be buried in a grand grave. The large stone structure has three arches on each side and is topped by a pyramid. Inside the mausoleum is a chest tomb. The inscriptions tell you that this holds the remains not only of Ralph Allen but also of his second wife and other members of the family. The last interment here was in 1993.

After more than two centuries, the monument had started to deteriorate and was in danger of collapse. However, a grant from the Heritage Lottery Fund allowed a full restoration in 2002. Two information boards were added at the same time. One relates the story of Ralph Allen and the British postal system; the other tells of his home at Prior Park and the quarrying of Bath stone.

Accounts differ as to who designed the mausoleum. Some say that it was the work of Robert Parsons, a local stonemason. Others favour Richard Jones, Allen's clerk of works, who was responsible for the Palladian Bridge at Prior Park. It is possible that they both had a hand in it.

More intriguing is the (unsubstantiated) story that Ralph Allen himself was involved in the design and that he was shown the plans a few days before his death. You might wonder why a philanthropist such as Allen, who was described by the poet Alexander Pope as 'humble', should have desired such an ornate memorial. Perhaps he liked the idea of being buried with his family all around him.

CLAVERTON PUMPING STATION

A rare piece of Georgian technology

Ferry Lane, Claverton, BA2 7BH
claverton.org
Open days during summer – see website for dates
Entrance charge
Bus D1 from Guildhall to Claverton Village, then 6-min. walk

The end of the Georgian period in Bath coincided with the beginnings of the Industrial Revolution. One place where a remarkable piece of Regency technology can still be seen is the Claverton Pumping Station.

The Kennet & Avon Canal was built in 1810 as an inland transport route for heavy goods. However, leakage from the canal meant that during periods of low rainfall the water level fell and boats were unable to pass through the lock flight in Bath. A way had to be found to top up the canal by moving water upwards from the River Avon.

© Rodw

The Claverton Pumping Station opened in 1813. It was designed by John Rennie, a Scottish engineer who was also responsible for the Dundas Aqueduct (see p. 284), and it was the only pumping station of its type in Britain. It was environmentally friendly, relying solely on the force of the river to turn a waterwheel and drive a pump that then transferred water up to the canal.

The pumping station remained in use until 1952, when falling canal traffic and the need for repairs made it uneconomic to maintain. It was replaced by a diesel pump and later by the current electric pump.

The historic pumping mechanism was restored in the 1970s and since

then it has been maintained by a team of volunteers. One job that needs to be done regularly is re-timbering the waterwheel – this was last carried out in 2012.

The Claverton Pumping Station is now a museum. On open days, the massive waterwheel turns once more and you'll be able to see the pump in action. You can also discover some industrial artefacts from the 19th century as well as a bit of social history. You'll hear the stories of the men – and their families – who worked as engine-keepers.

If you wonder why a waterwheel needed to be covered by a stone building, you'll learn that this was to save the inhabitants of the nearby manor house from the horror of looking at an industrial structure!

The easiest way to reach the pumping station is to walk along the canal. If you drive, note that there is no parking nearby – the best place to park is at Brassknocker Basin, a 30-minute walk away.

INDUSTRIAL HERITAGE AT DUNDAS AQUEDUCT

Where three waterways met

Brassknocker Basin, Monkton Combe, BA2 7JD
canalrivertrust.org.uk/places-to-visit/dundas-aqueduct
Bus D1 from Guildhall to aqueduct

Dundas Aqueduct is a magnificent spot in itself, a remarkable piece of engineering that carries the Kennet & Avon Canal across the River Avon. It also has several reminders of the area's industrial past.

The building of a canal in such a hilly region posed many challenges. Building aqueducts to carry water across the river was a way of keeping the canal level and thus avoiding the creation of numerous locks. Avoncliff Aqueduct opened in 1805 and Dundas was completed in 1810.

There was also a third waterway here, as this was where the newly created Somersetshire Coal Canal met the Kennet & Avon. It must have been a very busy place, with the regular loading and unloading of boats and the weighing of cargoes to calculate toll payments.

Although the boats you see here today are leisurecraft, quite a bit of industrial heritage remains. The Georgian toll house is where toll charges were calculated and paid, the fee being based on the weight of the cargo and the total distance travelled.

The stone blocks on the ground outside the toll house were part of the process for weighing cargoes. Empty boats would be loaded with the stones, and the boat's position in the water was measured. This measurement was then retained and compared with the height of the boat when fully laden. This enabled the weight of the cargo to be calculated.

The crane by the wharfside was used to load the stones and the cargo on and off the boats. It was manufactured by Acramans of Bristol and is thought to be the last of their cranes to survive.

Beside the wharf is the entrance to the old coal canal. Although this closed in 1902, a short section is still used as private mooring. Walk along the towpath to Brassknocker Basin and you'll come to a visitor centre with a small exhibition area and the Angelfish restaurant.

TURLEIGH TROWS

Water supply or sacred spring?

Green Lane, Turleigh, BA15 2HH
Train from Bath Spa to Avoncliff, then 14-min. walk

Walk through the village of Turleigh and you'll hear water gurgling by the side of the road. This is the Turleigh Trows, an ancient source of drinking water that has attracted many legends.

Turleigh is built on a band of limestone above a bed of clay, resulting in a series of natural springs, the most powerful of which feeds the Trows. What you see is a series of interconnected stone troughs through which water flows from the deep underground spring. Even on a dry day there is a plentiful supply of water here.

The water emerges at a constant 11°C and has provided drinking water for the village since early times. Most villagers – or their servants – would have come to the Trows for their water, but it was later piped directly to some of the wealthier households. At a time when fresh clean water was a scarce commodity, Turleigh's springs were used not just by the locals but also by farmers from the surrounding countryside for their livestock and their households.

The springs served other purposes too. The water was used for brewing and for washing woollen cloths, the wool industry at one time being a major source of local economic activity. And the force of the flowing water powered the Turleigh tannery mill.

A notice beside the troughs now asks visitors not to pollute the water in any way as it is still used to supply the village's ponds, gardens and livestock. As a result, it is crystal clear and almost good enough to be drunk today.

Given their antiquity, it is perhaps not surprising that the Turleigh Trows should have attracted myths and legends. Some say that this is a holy well or sacred spring, a claim boosted by the fact that the water flows through a series of seven troughs (seven being regarded as a mystical r.umber).

It is also said that the legendary King Arthur watered his horses in Turleigh after fighting a battle nearby. Presumably this was the Battle of Bladon – thought to have been fought at Bathampton Down – at which the Britons defeated the Anglo-Saxons.

And the stone troughs themselves? They are reputed to be old coffins, possibly of children.

FRESHFORD PILLBOX

Wartime defences on the River Frome

Freshford Open Field, Freshford, BA2 7WG
Train from Bath Spa to Freshford

Across the river from the Inn at Freshford is a large grassy space known as Freshford Open Field. Walk along the river a little way and you'll come to a red brick structure partly covered in vegetation. This is an old pillbox, a defensive structure from the Second World War.

By 1940 Britain was preparing for a German invasion and a national defence system was required. In addition to the coastal defences, the General Headquarters (GHQ) line was established, a series of 'stop lines' designed to impede the enemy advance. In many places the stop lines followed the route of existing barriers such as rivers and railways.

A total of 18,000 pillboxes were placed along the stop lines. These were a type of reinforced guardhouse, built from concrete with an outer layer of brick. They had narrow loopholes through which weapons could be fired. Like the one at Freshford, they were often placed close to bridges so that they could blow up the crossing if necessary.

Pillboxes were to be manned by volunteers from the Home Guard, people who could not join the regular army because they were working in essential occupations. In the event, the pillboxes were never needed because the feared invasion did not materialise. However, the structures remain of interest to military historians because they are the last permanent fortifications to be built in Britain.

Freshford, which is close to the point where the River Frome joins the River Avon, was at the meeting place of two GHQ lines. The Blue Line ran from here to Reading, and the Green Line was intended to defend Bristol. If you follow the Green Line along the river from here to Avoncliff, you will pass two further pillboxes.

The Freshford pillbox is of particular interest, however, because it is possible to go inside. Duck down to pass through the narrow doorway and you'll enter a gloomy space with light filtering through the gun slits. You can see the places where the guns would have been kept and you get a sense of just how uncomfortable it would have been to man the defences.

If you do go inside, be aware that you enter at your own risk. The pillbox is dark and cramped, a small reminder of the reality of the Home Front.

ELF AND FAIRY FORAY

Where the little people live

Long Wood, Claverton Down, BA2 7AE
Skyline tour bus from Laura Place to Flatwoods Road
bathnes.gov.uk/sites/default/files/sitedocuments/Streets-and-Highway-
Maintenance/FootpathsandPublicrightsofway/fdt_leaflet_22-8-14_final.pdf

As you walk between the trees of Long Wood, you may start to feel that you're not alone because this is where the fairies and elves live. Look carefully and you might spot their houses.

The woodland path is part of the National Trust's Family Discovery Trail, opened in 2015. The 3.2-km trail includes a woodland play area, nature activities and geocaches. However, it's the mysterious Elf and Fairy Foray that is likely to catch the attention of young – and perhaps not-so-young – visitors.

Over a stretch of 400 metres are 15 numbered doors set into the base of some of the larger trees. Each of these is home to an individual fairy or elf and you can scan a QR code to find out more about them. They have intriguing names like Avalon Fruitpip or Juniper Icewitch, but you might want to avoid North Pepperfly ('always full of good intentions but she can't resist a playful trick!'). There is even one fairy who has never been seen – perhaps you'll be the first to spot her.

Some of the doors are firmly closed, suggesting that the inhabitants are either asleep or away from home. Others may be ajar, offering a tantalising glimpse of the house within. You will know that the fairies have been there because glitter – or fairy-dust – is often to be seen scattered around the roots of the trees.

Bath Skyline Walk

The Family Discovery Trail is a section of the Bath Skyline Walk, which explores the natural setting that contributes to the city's UNESCO World Heritage status. The 9.6-km circular route follows the hills that surround the city and offers views from different perspectives. One of the best views is from Bathwick Meadow, looking across the Georgian city towards Lansdown Hill.

The Skyline Walk covers a variety of terrain and takes in landmarks such as the American Museum and Sham Castle (see p. 272).

WILLIAMSTOWE COTTAGES

Religious texts above the windows and doors

Williamstowe/The Avenue, Combe Down, BA2 5EG
Bus 2 from North Parade to Hadley Arms

Building houses for working men was a bit of a preoccupation in the 19th century, often undertaken – at least in part – for philanthropic reasons. The religious intent behind the construction of a group of houses in the centre of Combe Down seems clear: each has a biblical text carved into the stone above the doors or windows.

Ever since Ralph Allen opened his quarries to the south of the city, the labouring population of Combe Down had increased. The work was low-paid and insecure, and people needed somewhere to live. Allen himself – no doubt for commercial as well as humanitarian motives – built several workers' cottages (see p. 294) but many more were needed.

In 1884 Jane Williamson, the widow of William Williamson (vicar of Headingley in Leeds until 1863), commissioned the building of some new houses 'to provide comfortable homes for Combe Down working men'. They were built along the narrow lane known as Williamstowe and around the corner on The Avenue.

This was a double dose of philanthropy. Rent from the houses was used to establish two new orphanages in Widcombe: the Williamson's Orphan Home for Girls in Macaulay Buildings and a similar home for boys in Combe Down. Both were in use until the mid-20th century.

In fact, this was not a new venture for Mrs Williamson as she had previously founded an orphanage for boys and girls in Leeds before moving to Bath. She was obviously as concerned for her tenants' spiritual welfare as for their material well-being. A chapel was built on Williamstowe and each new house had a religious text carved in stone at the front. Presumably these were intended to focus the minds of the workmen as they returned home each day.

Today the chapel has gone and it is hard to spot the texts on the Williamstowe houses because many have been obscured by new extensions or conservatories. The best place to see (and read) the texts is on the group of larger houses on The Avenue.

RALPH ALLEN HOUSES IN COMBE DOWN

Early examples of industrial housing

De Montalt Place, Church Road, Combe Down, BA2 5JJ
Bus 2 from Dorchester Street to Combe Down School

Many of the houses in Combe Down were built to accommodate the quarrymen and their families who moved to the area in the 18th century. The very first houses in the village were the row known as De Montalt Place, on Church Road. They were built by the quarry owner Ralph Allen and represent an early example of industrial 'model housing'.

Building homes for the workers became widespread during the Industrial Revolution, a combination of philanthropy and hard-headed practicality. However, the idea was new when the De Montalt Place houses were built. Allen was known as a philanthropist but he must also have been aware that his workers would be happier and more productive if they were comfortably housed and close to their work.

In fact, the terrace of 11 houses was somewhat superior to ordinary workers' cottages of the time. They were two-storey Georgian houses designed by John Wood the Elder and built by Richard Jones, who lived in one of the houses himself.

Jones was Ralph Allen's foreman, who later became his clerk of works. He worked on Allen's mansion house at Prior Park and was probably responsible for his mausoleum at Claverton (see p. 280). He subsequently became the City Surveyor of Bath, so it was probably not unreasonable for him to have the best house in the terrace. This was at the centre of the row and was known as Dial House. It was distinguished from its neighbours by a classical pediment and a sundial. The pediment – which bears the date 1729 – is still there but the sundial has now disappeared.

Of course, there may have been yet another reason for the building of these houses. They were built from Bath stone and must have been a great advertisement for the Combe Down quarries!

You can find another group of purpose-built workers' houses at Ralph Allen Cottages, at the bottom of Prior Park Road in Widcombe. These are smaller houses and a plaque on the outside tells us that they were built by Ralph Allen around 1740 'to house his stone masons who worked nearby'. The cottages were conveniently sited close to the wharf on the River Avon from where stone was shipped to Bristol and elsewhere.

COMBE DOWN TUNNEL

Britain's longest cycling and walking tunnel

Access from Devonshire Tunnel, via Bloomfield Green, BA2 2AB
Bus 4a from St James's Parade to Bear Flat
Always open but tunnel lights switched off overnight

The Combe Down Tunnel opened in 1874 as part of the Somerset & Dorset Railway between Green Park and Midford. Trains no longer run here but it is now the longest cycling and walking tunnel in Britain.

The tunnel was dug deep into the hillside beneath Combe Down. At more than 1.6 km in length, it was the longest railway tunnel in the country without any interior ventilation. This, together with excessive humidity, made it hard for fumes to escape and contributed to a fatal crash in 1929. It was said that the sound of a phantom train which had haunted drivers since the tunnel was built was also a factor.

Whatever the reason for the crash, improved safety measures meant that the tunnel continued to be used without further mishap until the Somerset & Dorset closed in 1966. For many years the tunnel was sealed off but public campaigning led to its reopening in 2013 as part of the Two Tunnels Greenway. It was fully restored and – because it was very long and dark – lighting was installed all the way along.

Walking (or cycling) through the Combe Down Tunnel is a slightly bizarre experience. As you adjust to the gloom and the sound of dripping water, you start to notice that noise carries and that you can hear the far-off sounds of bikes wheeling along and joggers' feet pounding the floor. You may even sense the presence of that long-ago ghost train – it is probably best to avoid the tunnel at night when the lights are switched off …

The nearest access to the tunnel's northern portal is via Bloomfield Green and the smaller Devonshire Tunnel. Alternatively, you can approach the southern end from Tucking Mill viaduct.

Just outside the tunnel at the southern end is an information board explaining the geology of the area and how the tunnel was built between the sandstone and oolite levels. As you walk through the tunnel, note the areas of exposed rock and the crystalline formations on the walls created by water and minerals leaking through the porous rock above.

MINESHAFT ENTRANCE IN FIRS FIELD

Preserving a piece of social history

Firs Field Open Space, Combe Down, BA2 5EQ
Bus 2 from Dorchester Street to Hadley Arms

There is little visible evidence today of the quarries that once dominated the village of Combe Down. The tunnels have been filled in, the ground has been stabilised and houses have been built over the land. But at Firs Field you can see the site of the last remaining mineshaft on public land in the village. It has now been turned into a memorial to the industry, to the men who worked in it and to Ralph Allen, who developed the local quarries.

The story of Combe Down and quarrying is told at the nearby Museum of Bath Stone (see p. 300). But Firs Field is more of a living monument. It is the site of one of Ralph Allen's quarries, opened in 1729. This was a massive underground quarry, a maze of tunnels and caverns.

Allen planted the land above Firs Quarry with trees, apparently adding forestry to his extensive business interests. The plantation is long gone but at the centre of the field is a large self-seeded chestnut tree which stands at the entrance to the old mineshaft. In 2017 it was decided that this, together with the field, should be conserved as a part of local history.

The wall around the mineshaft was rebuilt and extended. It was topped by a circular bench, built – of course – from Bath stone and fashioned by local students of stonemasonry. The words 'Site of access shaft to Ralph Allen's stone mines – the stone that built Bath' are carved around the edge. And beneath them is the World Heritage emblem, a reminder that stone from Combe Down contributed to Bath's UNESCO status.

Around the field are three information boards, covering every aspect of quarrying in Combe Down. You can read about the stone itself, the men who extracted it and the stabilisation project. Then there is the effect upon the ecology of the area, including the now-protected colony of bats that roost in the cavern beneath the field.

Finally, look down at your feet as you walk in or out of Firs Field. At the end of the stabilisation project in 2009, a series of poems was commissioned as a celebration of Combe Down's quarrying heritage. One of these – a circular poem by Andy Croft – was carved into 12 separate sandstone slabs and placed at the entrance and exit gates.

33

MUSEUM OF BATH STONE

Discover the quarrying history of Combe Down

54A Combe Road, Combe Down, BA2 5HZ
museumofbathstone.org
See website for opening times; also open by appointment
Entrance charge
Bus 2 from Dorchester Street to Combe Down School

The story of Combe Down village is the story of Bath stone and of the men who quarried it. You can learn about both at one of the city's excellent small museums, the Museum of Bath Stone.

There are two separate strands to the museum collection. First, there is the history of quarrying in Combe Down from the 1690s to the First World War (with a side reference to the Romans, who were the first to extract stone from the hillside). The narrative here is that the Georgian city of Bath was 'built from underneath', using stone extracted from the hills around Combe Down.

Although we now associate the stone mines with Ralph Allen (see p. 280), there were at one time more than 200 individual quarries in the area. This led to the building of miners' houses and the creation of Combe Down as we know it today.

The second aspect of Combe Down's quarries relates to the recent stabilisation project. By the 1990s, it had become apparent that the tunnels and caverns created by quarrying had destabilised the whole area and that immediate action was necessary. This led to a massive programme of archaeological mapping, following which the mines were filled in and sealed off. An important part of this work was the preservation of the habitat of a colony of bats that had made their home in the tunnels.

The museum is small but packed with artefacts and information. Of course, there is stone. Some items are perfect and skilfully carved, but there are also some geologically interesting 'discards' containing what is thought to be fossilised coral. There are quarrying tools and photographs, and lots of information about extraction methods and the stabilisation project.

A particular item of interest is the large amount of graffiti recovered from the walls of the quarries. Some of this was created by the miners themselves but new drawings continued to appear until the tunnels were sealed. Two large pieces of graffiti are visible in the foyer and it is hoped that more will be on display in the future.

The collections are larger than the space can accommodate and the Museum of Bath Stone is constantly looking for ways of making more information available. Current projects include creating videos and adding QR codes to exhibits, allowing access to digital records. It is all part of the continuing story of Combe Down and Bath stone.

JEWISH BURIAL GROUND

34

Reminder of a vanished congregation

1 Greendown Place, Combe Down, BA2 5DD
bathjewishburialground.org
Occasional open days throughout the year
Bus 2 from North Parade to Mulberry Park

Little remains today to remind you that Bath once had a small but thriving Jewish community. But hidden behind a tall wall in Combe Down you'll find the graves of many who lived here in the 19th century.

Several Jewish families arrived in the city in the 18th century to provide goods and services for the wealthy tourists who had begun to descend upon the city. As their numbers expanded, they needed a place to bury their dead and a piece of land was purchased outside the city in 1812. Two synagogues (of which nothing now remains) were later built in the city centre.

The cemetery remained in use until the 1920s. By now the community was dwindling and the ground fell into disuse. But in 2005 the Friends of Bath Jewish Burial Ground was established, with the aim of restoring the site and preserving an important part of local history. Through their efforts, the surrounding wall has been renovated, the graves have been cleaned up and the names of those buried have been recorded. The Friends are also restoring the small caretaker's house in a corner of the plot to create an information centre.

Wandering between the gravestones today, you'll notice a marked lack of ostentation, reflecting the Jewish belief that everyone is equal in death. But note the inscriptions in Hebrew and English and the symbols carved on some of the stones.

Look for images of urns (representing descendants of the tribe of Levi) and hands held in a gesture of blessing (symbol of the priestly Cohens descended from Moses' brother Aaron).

Although you won't find anyone particularly famous here, one notable grave is that of Joseph Sigmond. He was a very early practitioner of dentistry in the city and patented his own dental cleaning powder.

Relatives of those buried in the Jewish Burial Ground may visit by arrangement. Others are welcome at open days or on the guided walks that take place throughout the year – see the website for details.

POPE'S WALK

A little-used footpath with legends and historic features

Runs between Perrymead and North Road, BA2 5AY
Bus 2 from Dorchester Street to Perrymead

Walk from North Road to Perrymead along the footpath known as Pope's Walk and you'll be treading an ancient route into the city. Not only is it a peaceful and little-used track, but it has several historic features and a couple of spooky legends.

Starting at North Road, the path winds its way downhill towards Perrymead. At first sight, it may seem uninspiring, passing an industrial site, but it soon opens into quiet woodland, far removed from the bustle of the city ahead.

The first item of interest that you encounter is an ancient boundary stone, marking the border between Combe Down and Lyncombe & Widcombe. This is also thought to have been the site of a moot tree. In Saxon times, this would have been a place where people assembled to discuss and agree matters of local importance.

Passing a series of more recent boundary stones, you come to what is perhaps the main feature of Pope's Walk: the Dry Arch. Also called Pope's Arch or the Rustic Arch, this old tunnel-like structure once carried a private carriageway across the path and through Ralph Allen's estate. This was one of many drives across his land, laid out to take advantage of the expansive views from the hillside.

Further down the hill you come to Perrymead Cemetery. This is the city's Roman Catholic burial place, and the site of the Eyre Chantry (see p. 306).

As you walk, with no sound apart from the birds in the trees and the crackling of twigs beneath your feet, you can ponder the history – and mystery – of the area. The name Pope's Walk is relatively recent, a reference to the poet Alexander Pope, who often visited Ralph Allen and helped to design his garden at Prior Park.

Earlier names included Blind Lane, Hanging Lane and Hangman's Lane. One legend tells of a horseman who rode beneath the low bridge and knocked his head off (presumably making him 'blind'). Another says that a rider's cloak blew up in the wind, then caught on the bridge and he was hanged.

These stories might account for the different names, although it might be argued that they simply refer to the trees that hung over the path and obscured the vision. Either way, the route is now reputed to be haunted. Perhaps that is why so few people walk this way.

EYRE CHANTRY

Elaborate mortuary chapel for the Eyre family

Perrymead Cemetery, Popes Walk, Perrymead, BA2 5AF
Open on Heritage Open Days and to groups by appointment (donation requested)
belindacarruthers@btinternet.com
22-min. walk from Bath Spa railway station

The Roman Catholic cemetery in Perrymead has two mortuary chapels, one of which is a private chantry for the Eyre family. A masterpiece of Gothic Revival design, it is still used for family burials.

For many years, Roman Catholic burials in Bath were at the church in Old Orchard Street (now the Masonic Hall, see p. 42). However, in 1856 a cemetery was opened in Perrymead to serve the new Catholic church of St John the Evangelist that had been built in North Parade.

The main chapel dates from 1859. The following year, John Lewis Eyre commissioned a private mausoleum for himself and his wife. The Eyre Chantry subsequently became a family burial place and many interments have taken place there since.

The Eyre family were a long-established Roman Catholic dynasty that originated in Derbyshire. John Eyre himself, who died in 1880, was a founding director of the London & South Western Railway company. He was also a prominent Roman Catholic who was known as 'Count Eyre', the title of Count of the Lateran Hall having been bestowed upon him by Pope Gregory XVI.

The chapel was built in the Gothic Revival style and the architect was Charles Hansom, a well-known designer of Catholic buildings. Several important manufacturers of church furnishings worked on the interior.

You can see the outside of the chapel at any time but it is the interior that is most spectacular. It might be small but it is intricately decorated. There are arches supported by marble columns, stained glass by Hardman Powell and a magnificent tiled floor. Perhaps the most eye-catching feature is the altar. This takes the form of a sepulchre, with an alabaster figure of Christ beneath a marble canopy.

The Eyre Chantry is now administered by a family trust. Although the crypt (where family members are still interred) is not open to visitors, you can see the inside of the chapel on Heritage Open Days. It is also open to groups by appointment.

MEMORIAL
TO EDDIE COCHRAN

Remembering a legendary rock star

St Martin's Hospital chapel, Midford Road, BA2 5RS
Bus 172 from bus station to Midford Road

O**utside a disused chapel in the grounds of St Martin's Hospital are two memorials. They are both to the same man: the American rock singer Eddie Cochran, who died here on 17 April 1960.

Cochran was just 21 when he flew to England for a four-month concert tour but he was already a music legend. He had had a string of hit singles, including the classic 'Three Steps to Heaven', and had appeared in a number of films. He had just played his final performance at the Bristol Hippodrome when – no doubt exhausted from a gruelling schedule – he made the fatal decision to take a taxi to Heathrow Airport so that he could fly back to the US the next day.

It was a long journey on a poor road late at night. Just as the taxi approached Chippenham, the driver lost control of the vehicle and it left the road. The passengers were taken to St Martin's Hospital in Bath but Cochran died the following afternoon. His companions, though seriously injured, miraculously survived the crash.

Eddie Cochran's many local fans arranged for a memorial sundial to be placed outside the hospital chapel on the spot where the casket containing his body rested prior to its return to the US for burial. A second memorial was created in 1998 and fully restored in 2010. This one is more elaborate and details Cochran's many claims to fame. Both memorials can now be seen beside the chapel.

There have been further local tributes to the singer. An annual Eddie Cochran Festival was established in Chippenham in 1995, and in the decades since his death many donations in his name have been made to the hospital that tried to save his life.

St Martin's Hospital occupies the grounds and buildings of the former Bath Union Workhouse (see p. 310). The chapel was built by John Plass, who lived in the workhouse and was apparently aged 78 at the time! Many of the workhouse residents were buried in the land around the chapel but – unlike Eddie Cochran – there is no record of their names and their graves are unmarked.

WORKHOUSE BURIAL GROUND

Where the poor were buried in unmarked graves

Wellsway, BA2 2UL
Bus 4 from St James's Parade to The Beeches

Between 1858 and 1899, more than 3,000 people were buried in unmarked graves in a field beside the Wellsway. Unlike others whose burial place is unidentified, these were not criminals or casualties of war. They were simply poor, having ended their days in the workhouse. But in recent years, campaigners have determined to create a lasting memorial to those whose names have been forgotten.

The Bath Union Workhouse opened in 1838. In those days, workhouses were the last refuge of those who could not provide for themselves. Many of the residents were elderly, sick or disabled but their numbers also included unmarried mothers and orphaned children. Conditions were grim, with hard physical work, terrible living conditions and rarely enough food.

It was possible to leave the workhouse if you managed to find employment or – in the case of children – if you were apprenticed to an employer. However, it was inevitable that many people stayed until they died and it was necessary to find space for burials.

The workhouse in Bath purchased two plots of land, one beside the chapel and the other in a nearby field, now known as the Workhouse Burial Ground. As many as 1,107 people were interred in the chapel plot and a further 3,192 in the burial ground. Whether for reasons of economy or simply because the people were considered unimportant, no effort was made to mark the graves or to record individual resting places.

Over the last few years, community groups and relatives of those who died in the workhouse have campaigned for proper recognition of the people buried here. There have been informal ceremonies, readings of the names of the dead and research into the lives of the workhouse inhabitants.

More recently, volunteers have planted the land – which is still consecrated – with bulbs and wild flowers. The hope is that it will become a wildlife haven and a fitting memorial to the dead. An information board has now been added, telling the story of the workhouse and the burial ground.

Standing at the edge of the ground today, you can just make out the mounds of individual graves. And, if you visit in the spring, you will see lines of daisies in the grass. It is suggested that these trace the edges of individual burial places – nature's own grave markers!

THE WANSDYKE

39

Remnants of an ancient earthwork

Combe Hay Lane, BA2 8PA
Bus 4 from bus station to Combe Hay Lane

Although parts of it can be seen elsewhere, little now remains of the Bath section of the Wansdyke. But a footpath to the north of Sulis Manor follows the route of this ancient earthwork.

We know that the Wansdyke was around 80 km long and that it was built in two sections. The West Wansdyke (of which the Sulis Manor section is a part) ran from the south of Bristol to Odd Down in Bath, while the East Wansdyke went from Devizes in Wiltshire to the Severnake Forest. An old Roman road linked the two.

We also know that it was a massive bank flanked by a ditch. The bank was up to 3 metres high; the ditch was around 5 metres wide and 3 metres deep. In Saxon times it was called Woden's Ditch: among other things, Woden was the god of tribal boundaries.

This is as much as we know for certain. We have no firm evidence as to who built the dyke, when it was built or even what it was for. The method of construction resembles the Roman military tradition but the dyke is not now believed to have had any military or defensive purpose.

Current theories place the building of the Wansdyke at some time between the 5th and 7th centuries, a period covering the late Roman era and the arrival of the Saxons. Given that it was probably created as a boundary, the chances are that it was designed to mark the dividing line between two Saxon kingdoms.

Most of the West Wansdyke has now disappeared and some of what remains is on private land. But you'll get an idea of what it would have looked like by following the footpath between Combe Hay Lane and Southstoke Lane (the start of the walk is close to St Gregory's College, not far from Odd Down Park & Ride car park).

Whatever its original intent, this section has been a boundary marker for more than 1,000 years. It now defines the northern edge of Southstoke parish. But the route may have been in use for much longer. The straight line it follows suggests that at this point the dyke may have been built on the site of an earlier Roman road.

The path follows the line of the top of the dyke. The ditch is full of trees and plants, the position of the treetops giving a clue to the depth of the ditch. Looking across to the roofs of houses behind the trees, you get a sense of how high up you are. There are also various points where you can walk down steps and look back to see the height of the dyke.

THE HOLES AT
ST PETER'S CHURCH

A squint for the benefit of lepers or for church officials?

Englishcombe, BA2 9DU
Bus 1 from Avon Street to Padleigh Turn, then 17-min. walk

40

St Peter's in Englishcombe is a charming Norman church, possibly with Saxon origins. As befits such an old structure, it has several interesting features. One of these is visible before you enter the church: two strangely shaped holes in the side wall of the entrance porch.

The porch was only added in Victorian times, so these holes would originally have been an outside window, allowing a view of the interior. They were what was known as a 'squint', or hagioscope, but why were they necessary?

A popular explanation is that the squint was for the benefit of lepers, who were not allowed inside the church. In the Middle Ages, leprosy was considered to be contagious and some people regarded it as a punishment for sin. So a squint would enable lepers to hear the Sunday sermon while remaining outside.

The problem with this theory is that Englishcombe is a rural location. Lepers were mostly restricted to communities on the edges of towns and could not roam the countryside at will. Infectious diseases were rife in the Middle Ages, however, perhaps it was necessary to stop people suffering from other maladies from entering the church and infecting the congregation.

An alternative, more practical reason for the squint has been suggested. It is possible that the window was there to allow a church official to see when Mass was about to start so that he could ring the communion bell.

In the absence of formal records, we will never know for certain. However, in the 21st century all are welcome to enter St Peter's. If you find the door closed, just ring the number shown on a window beside the door and a churchwarden will let you in.

Four military flags

A more modern curiosity are the four military flags inside the church. One of these is the Union Jack that was flying at Lüneburg Heath when Field Marshal Montgomery accepted the German surrender there in 1945. Montgomery presented the flag to St Peter's in 1947 but no one is quite sure why the church was so honoured …

MILLENNIUM VIEWPOINT

A spectacular hidden viewpoint

Manor Farm Buildings, South Stoke, BA2 7PQ
Bus 4 from St James's Parade to The Beeches, then 19-min. walk

Bath is famous for its viewpoints but the best-known of them look down upon the Georgian city itself. One place where you can find a different – but no less spectacular – perspective is at the Millennium Viewpoint on South Stoke Plateau.

South Stoke Plateau is at the southern end of the Cotswolds Area of Outstanding Natural Beauty, and it forms part of the natural setting included in the Bath UNESCO World Heritage Site.

The Millennium Viewpoint was created in 2000 to mark the turn of the century.

It occupies a small piece of land on the very edge of the escarpment and has a large semicircular stone bench where you can sit and admire the vista. It can only be reached on foot, so it remains hidden away and is mostly used by hikers and local dog walkers.

The escarpment falls sharply to reveal a landscape of gently rolling hills, farms and woodland. The Cotswolds give way to the Mendips on one side, and to the Wiltshire countryside – stretching all the way to Salisbury Plain – on the other. The viewpoint itself is ringed by trees and wild flowers and you are likely to spot kestrels circling above the open farmland.

A toposcope points out some places of interest. If you are planning to explore some 'secret places' further afield, you might note that three follies are visible from here: Alfred's Tower at Stourhead, the Ammerdown (or Jolliffe) Column near Radstock, and Cranmore Tower, the highest point on the Mendip Way.

You can walk to the Millennium Viewpoint from South Stoke village, Odd Down Park & Ride car park, or the Cross Keys pub. It might seem obvious to say that you should visit in daylight to enjoy the views. However, the lack of light pollution here is such that those who visit under cover of darkness will find some of the best star-gazing conditions in Bath.

LANTERN CROSS AT THE CHURCH OF ST JAMES THE GREAT

Ⓒ 42

An imposing memorial

South Stoke, BA2 7DT
Bus 4A from St James's Parade to Cross Keys, then 9-min. walk

The first thing you're likely to spot as you enter the churchyard of St James the Great at South Stoke is a tall column topped by a carved lantern head. This is a memorial to Lieutenant John Harman Samler, a casualty of the First World War.

Lt Harman was just 24 years old when his ship, the HMS *Queen Mary*, went down at the Battle of Jutland on 31 May 1916. The battle claimed more than 6,000 British lives, including almost all the crew of the *Queen Mary*. As this was a sea battle, many of the bodies were never found and those that were recovered were buried near Gothenburg in Sweden. Lt Harman's family did not have a body to bury but in 1931 his father, Rev. William Harman of South Stoke church, erected a cross in the churchyard in memory of his son.

The memorial was a copy of a 15th-century lantern cross, with a tall octagonal shaft on a shallow tiered base. The sculpture at the top is known as a lantern because it has four distinct faces. On one side is a carving of the crucifixion; on the opposite face is St James, to whom the church is dedicated.

Lantern crosses seem to have been common in Cornwall in the Middle Ages but more modern versions were often erected as war memorials. Although the South Stoke cross only bears the name of Lt Samler, it is possible that it was also intended as a more general memorial. Information inside the church states that it serves as 'a single memorial for all the dead buried here'. And the church's Roll of Honour – which pleasingly records the names of all those who served as well as those who died – shows that in the First World War, 67 South Stoke men went to fight but only 57 returned. So it seems fitting that they should also be commemorated.

While you're in the churchyard, have a look at the rather fine Norman arch around the main door. This dates back to c. 1170. Above the door is a modern carving of St James, surrounded by the scallop shell with which he is traditionally associated. This was created in 2000 by Derek Carr, a local sculptor, to commemorate the Millennium.

COMBE HAY LOCKS

How to carry barges uphill

Combe Hay, BA2 7NX
coalcanal.org
Bus 4b from St James's Parade to Cross Keys, then 25-min. walk

If you follow a steep downhill path from South Stoke to Combe Hay, you'll pass some old stone structures. These are the remains of the Combe Hay Locks, which once carried the Somersetshire Coal Canal up the hillside.

In the 18th century, coal was mined in the Radstock area and brought to Bath by horse-drawn road transport. But competition came in the form of coal from Welsh mines that could be more efficiently transported via the new Monmouthshire Canal. So Radstock had to construct a canal link of its own.

The Somersetshire Coal Canal was built around 1800 and ran between Paulton and Bath, joining the Kennet & Avon Canal at Dundas (see p. 284). However, a major problem arose when taking the waterway up the steep slope at Combe Hay, where it was required to climb more than 40 metres over a distance of around 2.6 km.

The first idea was to install three caisson locks, in which boats would be enclosed in a watertight chamber and hoisted up or down the hill. When the first of these was built, it was obviously regarded as a technological marvel – Jane Austen wrote in a letter that she was planning a visit to the new 'Cassoon' – but unfortunately it proved impractical.

The eventual solution was the creation of a flight of 22 locks, supported by a pumping station that would take water back up to the top of the hill. It must have been rather time-consuming to pass through so many locks, but the canal was remarkably successful. At one point it was transporting up to 100,000 tons of coal every year.

The canal remained in use until 1898. It gradually became derelict but in recent years the Somersetshire Coal Canal Society has been working on restoring stretches of the waterway, and parts of the lower flight of locks are now clearly visible.

Walk past the Combe Hay Locks on the Coal Canal Way today and you'll find yourself in quiet countryside, probably with no one else around. But try to imagine the place 200 years ago, when it was a hive of activity, with boats and bargees moving up and down the hillside and the water being pumped back up to the top.

MIDFORD STATION

An insight into a lost way of life

Two Tunnels Greenway, Midford, BA2 7DA
Bus D2 from bus station to Hope and Anchor

The Somerset & Dorset Joint Railway from Bath to Bournemouth (sometimes known as the 'Slow and Dirty') closed in 1966, despite public opposition. The section from Midford to Green Park is now part of the Two Tunnels Greenway, a walking and cycling route. At what remains of Midford station you can get a sense of how important the railway was to a small rural community.

There is little to see of the station itself apart from the platform and the foundations of the passenger toilets. But outside is a replica of the

timetable from 26 September 1949, giving a fascinating insight into the role of the railways in the mid-20th century. The timetable lists 'Passenger, Milk & Freight Trains etc' that seem to have run with astonishing frequency. We see that goods trains chugged their way through the night and that, whether you lived in the city or the countryside, you could rely on the trains to deliver your milk and your post.

A modern rail user might be astounded at the number of places to which you could travel. Apart from the major towns along the route, the trains stopped at small villages like Midford, which only had a few hundred residents. Look closer and you'll see that trains would occasionally travel further afield, to places like Bristol, Sheffield or Manchester ... although, given the number of stops, those must have been very time-consuming journeys!

Have a look at the notes too. On one train the guard had to 'collect tickets and extinguish Down platform lights'. There are helpful notes about the speeds of different trains and the times when signal boxes would be closed. It all helps to build a picture of a vanished world, giving a sense of the bustle on the platform with parcels and post being unloaded from the train, and passengers climbing on board with their suitcases, bound for the city or the coast.

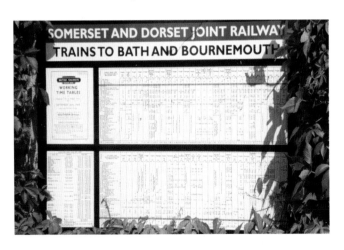

Midford station features in the opening scenes of the 1953 Ealing comedy, *The Titfield Thunderbolt*. Other locations for this film include nearby Monkton Combe station and the village of Freshford.

MONKTON COMBE MILL

New use for an old building

Mill Lane, Monkton Combe, BA2 7HD
Mendip Fireplaces showroom: Mon–Fri 10am–4pm
Bus D1 to Viaduct Hotel, then 13-min. walk

The village of Monkton Combe is now dominated by its public school, founded in 1868 to educate the sons of missionaries. But look closer and you'll find signs of earlier economic activity. These include the old mill, now repurposed for modern business activities.

In the Middle Ages, Monkton Combe was part of the lands owned by Bath Abbey and it was primarily agricultural. There were two grain mills, one in the village itself and one a kilometre away at Tucking Mill.

The area became more industrial with the opening of local quarries and the arrival of the Somersetshire Coal Canal. In the 19th century, a flock mill was built on the site of the medieval grain mill in Monkton Combe. Old clothes were purchased from rag and bone men and turned into flock for the stuffing of mattresses and other domestic items.

Power for the mill was generated by a waterwheel. However, the industrial process created a large volume of steam. A prominent feature of the new structure was the tall brick chimney, which remains visible from some distance away.

As you approach the mill, you can see that it was a sizeable complex of industrial buildings. If you walk around the back, you'll spot the remains of the sluice gates and the millpond (although the pond is now rather overgrown).

The flock mill remained in use until the mid-20th century, when it was sold and converted to alternative commercial uses. It now houses a number of different businesses. They are not all open to the public, but if you want to have a wander around the inside of the old mill you can visit the Mendip Fireplaces showroom.

Tucking Mill

The nearby Tucking Mill was used for tucking (or 'fulling'). This was a process of cleaning and thickening cloth by pounding Fuller's earth into the wool (Fuller's earth was extensively mined around the south of Bath).

However, Tucking Mill is perhaps better known as the home of William Smith, the 'father of English geology'. While working as a surveyor on the Somersetshire Coal Canal, he observed and recorded the strata in the rock and established the principles of modern geology.

FOSSILS AT STONEY LITTLETON LONG BARROW

Prehistoric building material

Stoney Littleton, Wellow, BA2 8NR
Car parking off Littleton Lane, or approx. 20-min. walk from Wellow

(46)

Set in the hilly farmland to the south of Bath, Stoney Littleton Long Barrow is worth a visit for many reasons. It's a peaceful countryside location just a few kilometres from the city centre. It's one of England's finest chambered tombs from the Stone Age. And the stones from which it's built contain lots of fossils, including a large ammonite strategically set beside the entrance.

Long barrows were a particular form of communal tomb from the Neolithic period. Particularly common in this part of England, they consisted of mounds of earth and stone with an internal passage leading to individual burial chambers.

The Stoney Littleton barrow was built around 3500 BCE. At 30 metres long, with several well-preserved chambers, it is considered one of the best – and most accessible – of such tombs in England. However, of particular interest is the stone it was built from, full of fossils from an even earlier period.

How far this was deliberate is hard to tell. It is possible that fossil-rich stone was just the nearest material to hand when the tomb was built. On the other hand, it is claimed that prehistoric people saw fossils as having particular significance or even magical powers.

Certainly the placing of a large ammonite on the left-hand side of the entranceway looks deliberate. The spiral shape has been treated as mystical across all ages and cultures and is often found on tombstones, perhaps symbolising life or life beyond death. Our prehistoric ancestors may have wanted to show the purpose of the tomb or to provide a talisman for the protection of those within it.

We will never know for certain, but if you enter the tomb you might just feel some of the magic conferred by the fossils around you. Note that you will need to duck your head, or even crawl, to get to the end of the passage!

You can access the barrow via a small car park beside the road at Stoney Littleton Farm. Alternatively follow a footpath from the village of Wellow, around 1.5 km away. However, you need to be aware that this path is often very muddy and waterlogged, and boots or wellingtons are advisable.

CAMERTON BATCH NATURE RESERVE

Where coal mining shaped the landscape

Red Hill, Camerton, BA2 0PB
camertonparishcouncil.co.uk/camerton-batch-lnr
Bus 174 from bus station to Skinner's Hill, then 23-min. walk

Historically the Bath area was more associated with stone quarrying than with coal mining. However, the village of Camerton was at the eastern edge of the North Somerset Coalfield and evidence of its mining history is still visible at the Camerton Batch Heritage Trail.

Coal mining in Camerton goes back to Roman times. Extensive extraction only began at the end of the 18th century, when deep coal was discovered. Two pits were sunk. The Old Pit ceased production in the 1890s but the larger New Pit stayed open until 1950.

Nature gradually reclaimed the land and in 1987 the local council purchased the Old Pit Batch from the Coal Board (the name 'batch' refers to the slag heaps left over from the mining activity). It was designated as a nature reserve ten years later, and a heritage trail was built through the woodland.

The site entrance is at the former pithead, with a capped mineshaft visible in the ground. Display boards give information about the reserve and about Camerton's mining history.

Your attention will be caught by the large statue of a coal miner. This is one of two sculptures created for the Festival of Britain in 1951 (the other is now at the Big Pit National Coal Museum in Wales). A plaque beside the statue tells us that it was purchased for the village by CHL Kendall & Sons, a local builders' merchant, 'as a tribute to Harry Kendall and all the miners who worked in these coalmines'.

Follow the path around the woods and you'll see how the mine shaped the landscape. Your walk takes you over the old spoil heaps and there are tiny fragments of coal beneath your feet.

When you climb up to the highest point you come to another interpretation board. Although they have long disappeared at this point, you can see where the Somersetshire Coal Canal – and, later, the Bristol & North Somerset Railway – would have run, taking coal from Camerton to factories and homes in Bath. The shape of the mining landscape remains but it has now given way to trees and wildlife.

Thomas Jonglez

It was September 1995 and Thomas Jonglez was in Peshawar, the northern Pakistani city 20 kilometres from the tribal zone he was to visit a few days later. It occurred to him that he should record the hidden aspects of his native city, Paris, which he knew so well. During his seven-month trip back home from Beijing, the countries he crossed took in Tibet (entering clandestinely, hidden under blankets in an overnight bus), Iran and Kurdistan. He never took a plane but travelled by boat, train or bus, hitchhiking, cycling, on horseback or on foot, reaching Paris just in time to celebrate Christmas with the family.

On his return, he spent two fantastic years wandering the streets of the capital to gather material for his first 'secret guide', written with a friend. For the next seven years he worked in the steel industry until the passion for discovery overtook him. He launched Jonglez Publishing in 2003 and moved to Venice three years later.

In 2013, in search of new adventures, the family left Venice and spent six months travelling to Brazil, via North Korea, Micronesia, the Solomon Islands, Easter Island, Peru and Bolivia. After seven years in Rio de Janeiro, he now lives in Berlin with his wife and three children.

Jonglez Publishing produces a range of titles in nine languages, released in 40 countries.

Follow us on Facebook, Instagram and X

ACKNOWLEDGEMENTS
Thanks to the very many people who have shown me around the places in this book and shared their knowledge and insights with me. Particular mention must go to Amy Frost of the Bath Preservation Trust, Kirsten Elliott of the Akeman Press, and Stuart Burroughs of the Museum of Bath at Work. And special thanks to my husband Lawrence for accompanying me on my explorations of the city and the surrounding countryside.

PHOTOGRAPHY CREDITS
All photos are by the author except:
St Stephen's Church © Alastair Chalmers
Museum of Bath Architecture © Bath Preservation Trust
Museum of East Asian Art © MEAA

The photograph of the Herschel Museum is included courtesy of the Bath Preservation Trust
The map of the city walls is provided courtesy of Akeman Press

Author photograph by Liz Green

Maps: : **Cyrille Suss** – Layout: **Emmanuelle Willard Toulemonde** – Copy-editing: **Jana Gough** – Proofreading: **Lee Dickinson** – Publishing: **Clémence Mathé**